365 Days ~ 2

365 DAYS

By Frank Colacurcio

365 Days ~ 4

By **Frank Colacurcio**

With Jeanne Halsey

ISBN 978-1-105-49886-2

365 Days by Frank Colacurcio; with Jeanne M. Halsey. ISBN 978-1-105-49886-2. Copyright © 2012 by *Frank Colacurcio Ministries.* Published by *Precious Messenger Publications*, a division of *Frank Colacurcio Ministries.* This book is protected under the Copyright Laws of the United States of America; all rights reserved under International Copyright Law. No part of this book may be reproduced or transmitted in any form or by any means, electronic or mechanical, including photocopying, recording, or by information storage and retrieval system, in any manner whatsoever, without express written permission of the Author, except in the case of brief quotations embodied in critical articles and reviews.

Unless otherwise stated, all Scriptures quotations are taken from the Holy Bible, New International Version ®; copyright © 1973, 1978, 1984, 2010 Biblica; used by permission of Zondervan. Quotations from Scripture taken from The Message; copyright © 1993, 1994, 1995, 1996, 2000, 2001, 2002; used by permission of NavPress Publishing Group.

Printed in the United States of America.

For more information, contact:

Frank Colacurcio Ministries

Mosaic Christian Church

4430 Granite Drive

Rocklin, California 95677

United States of America

916.632.8600

www.365-days.org

Table of Contents

Foreword by Jeanne Halsey 11
Introduction 15

Spiritual Antenna 21
Showing God's Glory 31
Reaching Outward 39
Sustaining 365 Days 51
#1 - Prioritize Your First Love 57
#2 - Feed Your Faith 73
#3 - Do Not Worry About Tomorrow
.... 89
#4 - Keep Doing Good 95
#5 - Defend Yourself 111
#6 - Do Not Walk Alone 121
#7 - Do Not Grow Weary 129
#8 - Pick Sides 143
#9 - Always Remember: *"There's No Place Like Home"* 159
#10 - Document the Journey 165
The Jonah Dilemma 175

Postscript 203
Acknowledgements 209
Dedication 211
About the Author 213
Other Titles 217

Foreword

By **Jeanne Halsey**

"What is this book about?" you may ask. *"Is it like starting a fitness or dieting program, just with a spiritual application? Is it to teach us how to journal effectively, or what?"*

365 Days is a book determined to make us better disciples of Jesus Christ, empowered by our mutual love – He Who loved us first! Whether you are a new believer or have been walking with Christ for many years, we all need refreshing with these fundamental truths, which Frank has wonderfully presented through *365 Days*.

I am so proud of Frankie! In 1989, our family first met the Colacurcio family at a small church in Washington State, and we instantly connected on many levels: Frank's wife Dyan and I found ourselves "kindred spirits" ... their daughter Brook was our son Alex's "best-friend-who-is-a-girl" ... my husband Kenneth and I had an immediate ability to share our passion for Jesus Christ and His Kingdom with Frank and Dyan. Whether ministering in public or behind-the-scenes, we all flowed like perfect teammates. Our hearts were knit together, then and forever.

The Colacurcios then moved to California, and our encounters became infrequent but always enjoyable. Staying in touch by long-distance can cool a friendship, but that was not the case with us. When Frank phoned one day and asked me to help him get this book written and published, it was the most natural thing to do. However, I was in for a surprise.

I have been a Christian my whole life, yet I realized I was in danger of allowing my "first love" to become faded and worn-out. As Frank described the "365 Days vision" on the phone, and as I dived into the shaping of this book, it was a delightful experience for me. I lost elements of exhausted tarnish on my daily witness and gained much-needed strength in my daily accountability before God – I learned afresh how to let God speak **to** me and how to let God speak **THROUGH ME** every day. The talented woman who transcribed the raw materials for this book, Marisa

Nyman, also found Frank's perspective and insights transforming.

It is not possible for me to participate in a writing project I cannot personally endorse or practice. I wholeheartedly recommend *365 Days* to you!

Jeanne Halsey
Blaine, Washington
January 2012

Introduction

Do you remember June 16th, 2010? Unless that is your birthday or some special event, it was probably just another day. One of the 365 days you lived that year. But what if God's intention was for that day to be so more?

What if God had **great** plans for that day – memorable plans, plans worth living, plans that changed your life? Plans that somehow – through the business of Life and the demands of the day – slipped away unnoticed? Would you want to make sure that mundane, unimportant kind of day never happened again?

This book is about taking back your life and living it the way God intended you to live: every day one-day-at-a-time.

The Daily Grind

God never intended any of our days to become part of the daily grind. A daily grind that turns into weeks, then into months, then into years, then turns into a lifetime.

Every day was meant to be lived individually, intentionally, with purpose and passion. Every day was meant to be lived with the understanding that we will never get a chance to live it again.

Every day was meant to be lived with the understanding that it will only exist once in our lifetime – never to be retrieved, only remembered. We will never get a chance to take another shot at it, we will never get a do-over. Today is tomorrow's history.

God intends every day to be a gift, not a grind. But it does not usually turn out that way, does it? One day starts to run into another. Then we start having good days and bad days. Then we have a couple of bad days back-to-back. Before we know it, we are back in the daily grind again ... and our goal simply becomes survival.

This book is about changing all that. This book is about taking our lives and living the way God intended us to live, about seizing our future and choosing to live every day one-day-at-a-time! God wants us to wake up every morning expecting Him to do something IN US and

THROUGH US to reach out and touch those around us. *"This is my day to hear from God, and to be used by God!"*

We should start each day with our spiritual antenna up, looking to God and asking, *"What are You going to do IN ME today? What are You going to do THROUGH ME today? Who are You going to use to speak into my life? Into whose life are You going to speak THROUGH ME?"*

We cannot just lump our days into weeks, our weeks into months, our months into years – and call that our lifetime. We were never intended to live our lives a year at a time, a month at a time, or a week at a time – God intended for us to live our lives ONE DAY AT A TIME! **We need to live each day like we will never get it back!** How do we do that most effectively? That is what this book is about!

In some parts of this book, I have broken from tradition and written it in first-person present-tense, to help you understand that this is a book about TODAY. And because this book is about you and about me, I have written "we"; I am not being pretentious – only choosing to engage both of us. I have also changed names "to protect the innocent." Let this book be the key that ignites your life, living each day with purpose.

Frank Colacurcio
Rocklin, California
January 2012

Spiritual Antenna

Richard at Walmart

It is just after lunch. My wife Dyan and I have to go to Walmart. I really dislike Walmart. I do not hate it because it is a bad store – we shop there, it is a great place to buy – but I hate big buildings with big crowds. I just want to get in and get out. But this day is different: I am living like I will never get it back. This day is a one-of-a-kind, no-second-chances day. My spiritual antenna is up and I am watching.

As I near the Prescriptions department, I notice a man waiting in line at the counter. His appearance is disheveled: messy hair, oversized coat – like a man standing on any corner in any major city with a sign that reads: *"Will work for food. God bless."*

At first I start to walk right by, but then I turn around to look again ... and our eyes meet. I am thinking, *"This guy looks so familiar."* We stare at each other for the longest time, then I realize, *"He probably thinks I am a stalker."* But I keep looking at him, and then I start walking towards him. I see him say something to the guy next to him, and then he begins walking towards me.

By the time we finally come together, I know exactly who he is. I am not going to tell you his real name because I'm going to tell you his story; for now, I will call him "Richard."

I knew Richard many years ago when I was serving as an elder at a church in Washington state. Richard was a young man whom we led to the Lord at this church. He attended for about five years, eventually serving as a deacon. Then one day he told us he was moving his family to Alaska, and after that we lost contact. Eventually my family and I moved to California, and we never heard from him again.

That is, until this afternoon. On this one-of-a-kind, once-in-a-lifetime day at Walmart, of all places. After an awkward reunion, Richard starts to pour out his story to me.

"Frank, when my family and I moved to Alaska, things went okay for a while. Then a storm came into my life. I did not understand it. I did not know where it came from. I did not know who to blame, but I ended up blaming God. I thought He let me down. He broke my heart. I got mad at Him. I rejected Him. I held Him responsible for everything that was happening. I walked away from Him, and never looked back."

I am thinking: *"I cannot believe how he is literally pouring out his life, right here on Aisle 4 in Walmart."*

"Frank, the last ten years of my life have been hell," Richard continued. "I lost my wife. I lost my kids. I became addicted to prescription painkillers." (He had been standing in line for painkillers, using a stolen prescription he had bought on the street.)

"I woke up in my trailer this morning and I was out of drugs ... and out of hope. For the first time in ten years, I called out to God. Shaking, I got down on my knees, and said, 'God – if You really are the God You say You are, the God I met ten years ago – then prove it to me today. Do something impossible to show me that You love me.'" (At this point, Richard is openly weeping in Walmart.)

"Frank, when I saw you out of the corner of my eye, I thought you were a ghost. As I started to walk toward you, I realized it really was you. God is answering my prayer."

Right there, in Aisle 4, next to the *Nilla Wafers* boxes, I pray for Richard. It doesn't matter who is watching – it does not matter what they think. God is using me in Richard's life, and I am not going to miss my chance.

That, my friend, is what I mean by *living* **365 Days** – One-Day-at-a-Time, expecting God to do a work in us and through us at any moment.

"God, What Do You Want Me to Do Today?"

If I was not operating with my spiritual antenna raised – if I was not motivated by the recognition that this day is One-of-a-Kind-Day, a day I will never get back – perhaps I would not have recognized Richard. When I woke up that morning, my first words were: *"God, come on, show me! What do You want to do in my life today? What do You want to do through my life to care for someone else?"* I was living with my spiritual antenna up.

When I began living the principles of *365 Days*, my whole perspective changed. I activated my spiritual antenna, all my senses tuned to the Spirit of God, and I learned to **watch** for opportunities to minister, to **listen** for conversations to use my spiritual gifts, to **reach** for circumstances where God could work THROUGH ME.

Life is Not a Renewable Resource

365 Days is looking at life as having 365 individual, non-retrievable days in which God wants to do a work **in us and through us.** God has a specific intention for our lives, a plan and a purpose for every one of us. Finding that purpose each day will dramatically change our lives ... if we choose to be transformed. The question is: "Will we join Him in His plan?"

What would you answer if I asked you, "How many days are in an average

American's life?" In an unscientific survey at our church, we got these responses:

* 12% thought we have an average of 10,000 to 20,000 days of life expectancy
* 30% thought we have 20,000 to 30,000 days in our lives
* 30% thought 30,000 to 40,000 days
* 28% said 40,000 to 50,000 days (that is, collectively, 58% who think we have more than 30,000 days of life (a lot of days!)

The truth is: the average American will live to 77.6 years, or 28,324 days. That's not nearly as many days as most of us think we have. Because we are all alive and reading this book, it stands to reason that some of our days have been used up. Consider these statistics:

* If you are 20 years old, you only have 21,024 days of life left
* If you are 30, you have 17,374 days left
* If you are 40, you have 13,724 days to go

* If you are 50, you have only 10,074 days left
* If you are 60, you have 6,424 more days of life
* If you are 708, you have 2,774 days of life
* And if you are 80, you are already dead! Or at least, "Mostly dead" (as Miracle Max said in *"The Princess Bride"*

All kidding aside, what is the point?

The point is we need to realize we have a limited number of days here on Earth. Whether you are on the front end of your life, midway or pulling up the rear, you have a limited number of days on Earth. Our lives are not a renewable resource. Every day is a one-of-a-kind, never-to-be-lived-again, no-do-over-kind-of-day. Each day is absolutely valuable and absolutely important, and has a purpose in God's eyes. From His perspective, there are no wasted days – only days we waste.

God wants to do something in our lives, and He wants to use us to do something in somebody else's life. Too easily, we are distracted or discouraged. We are so self-centered or into the daily grind that we do not recognize how important every single day is.

What if we wake up every single day with expectancy? What if we start every day asking, *"What are You going to do in my life today, Lord? How are You going to use me in somebody else's life?"* This expectancy changes our lives from the *"same old, same old"* to making every day a great adventure, a day planned and purposed in Heaven.

Can you imagine how much it would change our lives if we start living like this one single day at a time? Looking for God to do a work IN US and THROUGH US each day? It would forever impact our lives and the lives of those around us.

Showing God's Glory

There is this envelope in Forever called Time. God had to invent Time just to redeem us. We think Time has always existed, but that is not true. Eternity has no beginning and no end. Eternity has always been – you can go back forever, and you can go forward forever – but there is no starting point or ending point that would create Time.

God created a beginning and called it Time (which does have an end). It is into this envelope of Time that He has placed the history of Man.

> *Then God said, "Let Us make Man in Our image, in Our likeness, so that they may rule over the fish of the sea and the birds of the sky, over the livestock and all the wild animals, and over all the Earth, and over all the creatures that move along the ground." So God created Mankind in His own image, in the image of God He created them; male and female He created them.*
> **Genesis 1:26-27**

God put Man into this envelope of Time to redeem the most precious thing He ever created: we who are created in His image and likeness. God created this envelope in history to send His Son down to Earth to die on a cross, to redeem us from the mess that Adam and Eve started – and every single man, woman and child have done since – which is sin.

God never wanted Time. His plan in the Garden of Eden – where He walked hand-in-hand with Adam and Eve – was to have intimacy and fellowship with His creation, Man. When Adam and Eve sinned, God didn't give up on us: He sent Jesus, His own Son, to **cleanup,** so we could **step up** into Eternity, and **live up** to the plan He had for us all along.

Why? To bring us back what He always planned: which is Eternity in His presence. That is the greater good. We tend to think of our lives as being all about us – our comfort, our good. God tends to think of our lives as all about His Kingdom, demonstrating faith in God regardless of our circumstances.

Let me show you what I mean.

Trust in Good Seasons and Bad

Sometimes there are bad things in our lives. Can we trust Him for that? Can we believe that a loving God is more interested in our character and developing our faith than He is about our comfort, our "perfect lives"? Can we find Him even in the midst of the storm, in the time of crisis, when things are not fair?

Some things happen because we live in a fallen world, where sin has entered.

> *He causes His sun to rise on the evil and the good, and sends rain on the righteous and the unrighteous.*
> **Matthew 5:45b**

Yes, God can discipline us in different ways, to correct us. Ultimately, He is a loving Father. It is important to know when we are being disciplined and when we're not. We are living in a fallen world, and God wants to show His glory and power through events in our lives.

Watching for opportunities for us to demonstrate the work of God displayed in us is the meaning of 365 Days.

Ripe For God to Move

In John 9, Jesus told His disciples that the man was blind, not because of his sin or the sin of his parents but because of the fallen world where we all live. He added:

> *This happened so that the works of God might be displayed in [the blind man].*
> **John 9:3b**

The blind man was not having a happy life, but he was ripe for Jesus Christ – the Man Who practiced 365 Days better than anyone else – was there on the scene.

"Maybe God does not want to use me," you might say. It is not that simple.

> *As long as it is day, we must do the works of Him Who sent Me. Night is coming when no one can work. While I am in the world, I am the light of the world.*
> **John 9:4-5**

"As long as it is day" – or "as long as I am alive here on Earth" – *"we must do the works of Him Who sent Me."* This is the outward part of 365 Days Living: doing the work of the Father. *"Night is coming"* – meaning Death – *"when no one can work."* When we die, the number of our days runs out and we are done. There are no more 365 days. We have a limited number of opportunities to be used by God. Our life spans are the "daytime" – each 365 days for every year we are alive.

When Death comes, we can no longer do any work. Jesus is saying, *"I am here for a season to work, to do the will of My father. But then night (death, His crucifixion) is coming, and I will not be here anymore to do the work. I am going to move on to Heaven ... and guess who takes over for Me?"* Jesus left us to take over His work. Every year of our lives, we have 365 individual opportunities to step into Jesus' shoes.

I am not talking about dying on a cross, because Jesus did that for us, conclusively – I am talking about laying down our lives and loving someone in Jesus' behalf. If we think for a moment that God does not want to use us, we are not reading the Book!

Go to your Bible, look up John 9:4-5 and highlight this: *"As long as it is day, **WE** must do the work of Him Who sent Me."* Jesus was looking at His disciples – and He is looking at us – and He said, *"WE."*

In Us and Through Us

"As long as it is day, we must do the work of Him Who sent Me" – one day at a time. Will we live expectantly, believing for God to do something **in** our lives, and to do something **through** our lives for someone else?

An effective way to practice 365 Days is to journal. This is one way to build up our expectations as we live 365 days a year for Christ. Journaling raises expectations, teaches and trains us where pitfalls may be. The enemy wants to kick the legs right out from under us, so we need all the tools we have to defeat our enemy and increase our impact.

I put my *365 Days Journal* right next to my bed, and write in it every night. When I wake up in the morning, there it is, reminding me that this is a fresh new day – not just "any other day" but my one shot at this day. God is on my side! He wants to do something special IN ME and He wants to do something special THROUGH ME.

God says, *"Frank, as you go through this day, I want you to meet with Me. Write down the things I say and the things I do in you and through you."* I start my day with my spiritual antenna up, my faith rising, expectant!

Failure should not have any weight in our lives. The way to bounce back from failure is yielding to the work of God in our lives, walking in a future we did not think was possible. If we have bad days – if we go off into sin, if we have failures – then we write in our Journals:

I am sorry.

It is a short entry that day. How much do you think that would change our lives? How much meaning would each day have? How much impact could every day have in our lives and in the lives of others around us?

Reaching Outward

Our lives are platforms. One thing I love to do is people-watch. It doesn't matter where I am – an airport, a grocery store, or in my own neighborhood – I love to watch people. The other day, my wife Dyan jokingly called me a stalker, but I quickly reminded her that Jesus liked to watch people too. I pulled out my iPhone and read Mark 12:41 to her:

> *Jesus sat down opposite the place where the offerings were put and **watched** the crowd putting their money into the Temple treasury.*

"See, Dyan," I said, "I am just like Jesus." Needless to say, the roll of her eyes was commentary enough, so I decided to let the sleeping dog lie.

Whether we know it or not, people all around us are watching too. They are listening to what we say, weighing what we do. They hear us over the fence, they see us at work or on campus, and they measure us when we are at our kids' sporting events. People love to watch people.

> *Ezra the teacher of the Law stood on a high wooden **platform** built for the occasion ... Ezra opened the book. All the people could see him because he was standing above them; and as he opened it, the people all stood up.*
> **Nehemiah 8:4-5**

God has given us a built-in **platform** called Life. With this platform comes an audience, and He wants us to take full advantage of the opportunities He provides.

> *Be wise in the way you act toward outsiders; make the most of every opportunity.*
> **Colossians 4:5**

God says, *"Your lives are being viewed by everyone around you, and I want you to make every moment count for My Kingdom! This means that living the 365 Days vision is not a ministry you have to add to your life – it is something you do right in the middle of your life! You already have the opportunity built in ... because your life is a platform for all to see!"*

All we have to do is wake up in the morning and start each day in faith, expecting and believing God to do a work **in us** and **through us!**

Think of it this way: we do not have to go out today and find someone to minister to – because everyone we are called to demonstrate Jesus to **is already in our lives right now.** They will be the people all around us – and make no mistake – they will be watching! This is God's given opportunity.

Listen to Gloria's testimony:

"Growing up, I was the 'rebellious child.' When I became an adult, I watched as my sister found Jesus and then continued to live for Jesus. I watched her for five years, and I finally became convinced that I needed Jesus."

Gloria saw Jesus in her sister, and what she saw was attractive and compelling. Her sister's platform won her to Christ.

Our Missed Focus

There is much anxiety in our lives and especially in the Church. We hear, *"We are in the end times"* – and that produces anxiety and confusion, a lack of focus in the Church. Christians are distracted and talking about things which have been clearly stated in Scripture but which we will never know the answer (at least, not here on Earth). Our daily life and focus are not to be on that.

> *Paul, Silas and Timothy: To the church of the Thessalonians in God the Father and the Lord Jesus Christ. Grace and peace to you. We always thank God for all of you and continually mention you in our prayers. We remember before our God and Father your work produced by faith, your labor prompted by love, and your endurance inspired by hope in our Lord Jesus Christ.*

> *For we know, brothers and sisters loved by God, that He has chosen you, because our Gospel came to you not simply with words but also with power, with the Holy*

Spirit and with deep conviction. You know how we lived among you for your sake. You became imitators of us and of the Lord, for you welcomed the message in the midst of severe suffering with the joy given by the Holy Spirit. And so you became a model to all the believers in Macedonia and Achaia. The Lord's message rang out from you not only in Macedonia and Achaia – your faith in God has become known everywhere.

Therefore we do not need to say anything about it, for they themselves report what kind of reception you gave us. They tell how you turned to God from idols to serve the living and true God, and to wait for His Son from Heaven, Whom He raised from the dead – Jesus, Who rescues us from the coming wrath.
1 Thessalonians 1:1-10

Paul the Apostle started a little church in a city called Thessalonica. He was there only three weeks, preaching in the synagogue. They started out really well, walking the walk and talking the talk. People in other places – like Macedonia and Achaia – were impressed with the

Thessalonians. Their faith, their ability to survive and thrive even when faced with persecution and suffering was like a model for all the other churches. Then they went off focus.

Misdirection and Misunderstanding

For the Lord Himself will come down from Heaven, with a loud command, with the voice of the archangel and with the trumpet call of God, and the dead in Christ will rise first. After that, we who are still alive and are left will be caught up together with them in the clouds to meet the Lord in the air. And so we will be with the Lord forever. Therefore encourage each other with these words.
1 Thessalonians 4:16-18

Somehow they misunderstood Paul's teaching. This Church thought Jesus was coming back any minute. They forgot what they were supposed to be doing as Christ's followers and instead focused on looking for and waiting for the return of Jesus. They neglected doing the work of Christ.

When Paul heard this, he wrote them a letter to correct and comfort them. That letter in the Bible is called First Thessalonians, written to the Christians in Thessalonica. If what is happening in the world today is undermining our faith – if we are nervous or worried – then jump into Thessalonians. This is how Paul calmed the Church and focused them.

> *They had misunderstood Paul's teaching. They were straining their eyes to catch, as it were, the first glimpse of their risen and glorified Savior returning in the clouds. Hence, the daily duties which pertained to the lives of Christ's followers, were neglected.*
> ~ **Barnes' Commentary**

They stopped living one day at a time, living with focus and purpose. They were so distracted with the return of Christ that they stopped living the instructions which Jesus gave in John 9:4: *"As long as it is day, we must do the work of Him Who sent Me."*

No one knows when Jesus is coming back, not even the angels. He is coming like a thief in the night – we never know when the thief is coming, which is why we get robbed. If we knew when he was going to show up, we would be there saying, "No way!" Jesus is coming, but we are not supposed to just sit down and wait for Him. We are supposed to be doing to the work of God, every day, like each day is going to happen just once and we can never repeat it.

"You are all sons of the light and sons of the day ... Live as sons." Be self-controlled, and wear faith and love like body armor, with the hope of salvation as a helmet. See your life as a platform in front of all those around you.

Living Every Day

Paul continues with instructions on returning to the things that God has called us to do, which is living every day, one day at a time, in Christ's shoes:

> *Now we ask you, brothers and sisters, to acknowledge those who work hard among you, who are over you in the Lord and who admonish you. Hold them in the*

highest regard in love because of their work. Live in peace with each other.

And we urge you, brothers and sisters, warn those who are idle, disruptive, encourage the disheartened, help the weak, be patient with everyone. Make sure that nobody pays back wrong for wrong, but always strive to do what is good for each other and for everyone else.

Rejoice always, pray continually, give thanks in all circumstances; for this is God's will for you in Christ Jesus. Do not quench the Spirit. Do not treat prophecies with contempt, but test them all; hold on to what is good; reject every kind of evil.

May God Himself, the God of peace, sanctify you through and through. May your whole spirit, soul and body be kept blameless at the coming of our Lord Jesus Christ; the One Who calls you is faithful, and He will do it.

1 Thessalonians 5:12-24

When we are living for a greater glory, living with a greater knowing of God inside, fear starts to slip away. Our faith increases and our fear decreases. As we begin to see God using us, our passion and fervency returns: *"I did it once, I can do it again!"* Once, we are reenergized ... twice, we begin to understand ... three times, we are on a roll ... four times, we are professionals!

- ✳ Live each day intentionally: on purpose for a purpose.
- ✳ Live each day strategically: choose the life we live.
- ✳ Live each day expectantly: expect God to do a work **IN US** and **THROUGH US.**

Sustaining *365 Days*

Before we can ever accomplish any goal, we must begin with the end in mind. We need a mental picture of what could be. Andy Stanley defines it as vision:

> *"Vision is a mental picture of what could be, fueled by a passion that it should be."*
>
> **~ Andy Stanley**

God redeems and restores our lives, overcoming our yesterdays ... but our tomorrows are a different thing – they have yet to be lived. God wants us to focus on our **todays,** learning to understand and believe that each day is as valuable to us as it is to Him. He looks at each of us and says, *"You will not believe what I have planned for you today!"* He cares so much about our individual lives and asks, *"Will you be as expectant as I am for your life?"* He has made promises and provisions in His Word for us to live much more than mundane lives.

God wants to work **in** us every day ... and He wants to work **through** us to help others every day. Do we believe this? Do we believe that God can use us, will use us and wants to use us in other people's lives every single day?

Remember what Jesus said:

"As long as it is day, we must do the work of Him Who sent Me. Night is coming, when no one can work. While I am in the world, I am the light of the world."

John 9:4-5

Jesus was using a metaphor for day and night. A "day" is a metaphor for our lives. In other words, *"As long as it is today – as long as I am alive, during My lifetime here on Earth, I must do the work of My Father."* Then He says, *"Night is coming"* – He will die, and He will no longer be here – *"so we must do the work of the Father."* Note: He says, *"We must do the work God sends us to do."* Every day, God is expecting **us** to be a part of that work.

In the very next line, Jesus says He is the Light. When Jesus left this world – after He died on the cross, was buried, was resurrected from the dead, had ascended to Heaven, to sit at the right hand of God – He never let us off the hook of being the "we" part of God's plan to continue His work. Who did He leave to take over His job? That is correct – us! We are the light of the world.

The world certainly is dark. We are the lights shining in the darkness:

> *You are the light of the world. A town built on a hill cannot be hidden. Neither do people light a lamp and put it under a bowl. Instead they put it on its stand, and it gives light to everyone in the house. In the same way, let your light shine before men, that they may see your good deeds and praise your Father in Heaven.*
> **Matthew 5:14-16**

> *For you were once darkness but now you are light in the Lord. Live as children of light.*
> **Ephesians 5:8**

It is God's intention for us – in the place of Jesus – to let His love shine through us, to **be** the light to the world. God wants to minister to us every day ... and He wants to minister through us every single day. *"God, come on, I am Yours! I am Your child today, and I want You to work IN ME, do something IN ME ... and I want You to work THROUGH ME."* This is living 365 Days!

Ten Steps of *365 Days* Living

You may ask, "How am I going to sustain being light to the world for 365 Days?" Here is my list, which I will explain one-by-one:

- Prioritize Your First Love
- Feed Your Faith
- Do Not Worry About Tomorrow
- Keep Doing Good
- Defend Yourself
- Do Not Walk Alone
- Do Not Grow Weary
- Pick Sides
- Always Remember: *"There Is No Place Like Home"*
- Document the Journey

365 Days ~ 56

#1 - *Prioritize Your First Love*

Every day when we get out of bed, we have to answer one question: *"Who are we going to love the most, ourselves or God?"* Why? Because whoever we decide to love the most is who we are going to live for on that day.

> *But seek **first** His Kingdom and His righteousness, and all these things will be given to you as well.*
> **Matthew 6:33**

When we committed our life to Christ, He became our First Love. Everyone and everything – ourselves included – immediately took their place behind Him.

The Battle Between Heart and Mind

Let us walk down Memory Lane for just a moment. Do we all remember the day or the moment when we made Christ our First Love? When we knew because we knew because we knew that Christ had died on the cross for **you and me?** That His death meant we live?

Oh, I remember that day like it was yesterday! February 6, 1984. *Lakewood Baptist Church*. The pastor's name was Ruffin Snow. He was from Oklahoma, and had the accent to prove it.

The previous year, I had been investigating the claims of Christ, and had finally been convinced of their truths just a few months earlier. I could not wait to receive Christ!

There was this one little hiccup in my plan: I had learned just enough about Jesus to know that if I invite Him in to be my Savior, I also invite Him in to be my Lord. My Master. The One Who is in control of my life, my whole life. I could not cut Him in half and take only the Savior part – He also wanted to be my Lord. He wanted to come in and clean out some of the stuff that had been hurting me.

The problem was that I was not living "a Christian life" at the time. To be exact, no one could even see any "Christian life" based on the way I was living. I was running nightclubs, and making a lot of money doing it. I liked the lifestyle this all afforded me. I had no intentions of giving all that up. So how could I accept Christ and still keep on running the clubs?

Is my dilemma plain? I liked the idea of trusting Jesus to save me, but I did not like the idea of relying on Him to support me, or even let Him control me. I had been doing just fine, and in grand style at that. In my heart, I knew the nightclubs would have to go if Jesus was going to come into my heart.

So I devised this plan which admittedly sounds a little silly now but at the time made perfect sense. I would diversify. I would get some money together, buy a few *McDonald's* franchises, and earn a lot of money in a way God could approve. Then I could keep my lifestyle and be a saved Christian at the same time. It was the perfect plan!

That is, until that Sunday morning, February 6, 1984, at *Lakewood Baptist Church*. The service was just about over, and like they always do in every Baptist church anywhere in America, the pastor was giving the invitation for folks to receive Christ. I had sat through many invitations like this one in the past few months. Every time, it was always the same – it was like there was a war going on between my heart and my mind.

My heart would be dying to go forward and receive Christ, but my mind would fight back, saying, "We **will** get saved ... just not yet. We have to diversify first." I would literally have to grip the pew, knuckles turning white, just to keep from going down the aisle. The war kept going on. Until this morning.

I was holding onto the pew with all my might, just waiting for the invitation time to end. Then it did ... or so I thought. The choir had just finished singing *"Just As I Am,"* and many people had responded and gone forward already. Then the pastor went to the microphone to close the service ... and he did the oddest thing.

He looked over the congregation and said, "Brothers and sisters, I believe there is war going on here today for someone's soul. So I tell you what we are going to do: we are going to extend this time of invitation. Choir, you sing one more verse of *'Just As I Am,'* and, brothers and sisters, you and I will pray, and we will see what God will do."

A double invitation! I never heard of a double invitation before! I half-expected to hear a buzzer and some referee saying, *"Foul, no double invitations allowed."* But there was no buzzer, no referee. I dug my fingernails into the pew. My heart started to explode with yet another opportunity to receive Christ ... but my mind fought back, shouting, *"Diversify! Diversify!"*

This time, my heart won. I could not resist the love of Christ for another moment. I could not live a minute longer without knowing Jesus as my Savior. I stood up, stepped into the aisle, walked to the front of the church, and kneeled down on the steps of the stage. There, with tears of joy and relief streaming down my face, I prayed to receive Christ as my Lord and Savior. Thus began the greatest love affair of my life.

Jesus, my Savior, my Lord, my **First Love.**

First Love First

That is what I am talking about in this first step toward sustaining 365 Days in our lives. We have to take a stroll down Memory Lane every morning. We have to remember Who is our First Love. We have to remember that God loved us so much that He sent His one and only Son to pay our debts. To die on a cross for us. His sacrifice, to pay for our sin.

Even as I write this, I cannot help but get excited thinking about it. I am not fooled because I know that when the alarm goes off morning tomorrow, the question will have to be answered again: *"Who are you going to love the most today, Frank – yourself or God?"*

You may be asking by now, *"Why every day?"* Because with the alarm in the morning will come the fullness of life, with all its demands and all its opportunities. Those demands and opportunities – our autopilot for self-preservation and self-satisfaction – will try to kick in. Warning sirens will go off: *"Danger, Will Robinson, danger!* What if God does not meet every need? What if God does not have a plan? What if God is not Who He says He is?" Suddenly that sick feeling of being left out on a limb comes in. Instead of trusting Him, it is easier to trust ourselves ... and without even realizing it, we move ourselves into the number-one spot. We decide to love ourselves and our plan for our day, instead of loving God and trusting His plan for our day.

> *Yet I hold this against you: you have forsaken the love you had at first.*
> **Revelation 2:4**

Plain and simple. Our faith will be challenged every day of our lives. If we are to live 365 Days every year for Christ, we must prioritize Him as our First Love every morning.

> *Yet I call to mind and therefore have hope: because of the* Lord*'s great love we are not consumed, for His compassions never fail. They are new every morning; great is Your faithfulness. I say to myself, "The* Lord *is my portion; therefore I will wait for Him."*
> **Lamentations 3:21-24**

The Throne of our Hearts

Our youngest son Jade Gabriel has *Downs Syndrome.* Some would say he is handicapped, but he does not think so. He just looks at Life simply. He understands Life simply, and he understands Love simply. When he tells you he loves you, he says it in the most simple way: he says, *"I love you in my heartbeat."* He understands that our hearts are where we decide who and what we will love the most. *Cardia* – the Greek word for "heart" – means "the throne of your affections." Only we get to decide who sits on the Throne.

To choose or prioritize our love, we say, *"Today, God, You are on the throne. I am not going to let myself on the throne."* This way, when we are at work, God is at the center of our lives. When we are folding the laundry, God is at the center of our lives. When we are walking in the hall between classes at school, God is at the center of our lives. When we are sitting at the airport between flights, God is at the center of our lives. We have just increased the chances of God moving through us when He is on the throne in every dimension of our lives! If we do not, we will default back to loving ourselves. God wants to move in us and through us every day.

Excuses, Excuses

Marilyn is at the grocery store and a woman behind her is having a rough time. Her kids are unruly and fighting, she is embarrassed, and looks beat down. God says inside, *"Come on, Marilyn, throw a little love her way. Be Jesus to her. Just encourage her. It is simple – say, 'How are you? Can I help you?'"*

Marilyn mutters, *"Wait a second, God, You know I do not do that sort of thing! I am an introvert, not an extrovert! I do not talk to strangers. Extroverts like Pastor Frank may do that, but not me. Remember how You made me: uniquely wired and knit together as an introvert! I do not do that. Be Jesus to other people? I am not going to invite someone to church. I am not going to serve my neighbor. I am not going to step out of my comfort zone."*

Sorry, Marilyn, but this Gospel says that when Jesus ascended into Heaven to sit at the right hand of God, He left every one of His followers to walk in His shoes, to take

His place as light to the world. There is no such thing as, "I just do not do that. That is a little too bold for me. I am an introvert." God wants to minister **through** us – every one of us who claims Jesus Christ as our Lord.

Not too long ago, I was taking our son Connor to a school in Auburn, California. I had to hurry down the interstate highway to get him to the bus station. As we were driving along, we saw a man (I will call him "Ben") pushing his broken-down car on the side of the road, about two miles from the exit. When I saw Ben's predicament, Holy Spirit said, *"Come on, Frank, be Jesus to this guy. Hop out and help him push his car."*

Then Frank (me, of course) said, *"Wait a second! How can I do that? If Connor misses the bus, I will have to drive him all the way to Auburn. Then I will be late getting back to the office, and somebody is going to be sitting there waiting, thinking, 'Hmm, Frank cannot even come to this meeting on time.' So do not tell me to stop everything and help this man!"* In my mind, I justified myself right out of being Jesus to Ben.

What was I really doing? I was loving myself. Do I really think someone was waiting in my office who would be upset if I walked in and said, "Sorry I am thirty minutes late, but there was a guy with a broken-down car and I helped push his car to the side of the road, and I knew you would not understand that." The fact is: I blew it. I had not decided that morning who was going to be my First Love, Who was going to be the center of my life that day. So, by default, who was it? Frank.

We have a million reasons why we put ourselves in first place, why we consider ourselves our first love. When we do not establish God in His rightful first place on a daily basis, we fail.

Maybe God put Ben with the broken-down car there on purpose: for me to minister to him. Maybe he was having challenges in his life, maybe this was his last straw. Maybe his marriage was on the rocks, or his kids were off in no-man's land, or he just lost his job. Maybe he was like Richard in Aisle 4 at Walmart, who asked God for one last sign that He cares.

Maybe Ben was saying, "Why do I even bother?" Then his car broke down ... and all he needed was for one person to say, "Hey, God has your back on this. He cares about you. He has a brighter tomorrow planned for your life."

Opportunities Not to Be Missed

Look at it the other way. Let us say it is you and me on the side of the road with a broken-down car. If we have prioritized God as our First Love, then everything becomes an opportunity! Rather than being stressed and worried – *"Man, I am going to be late! This car does not have a jack and I do not know how I am going to fix it"* – instead we say: *"This could be cool! God, what are You going to do? Are You going to work IN ME? Are You going go show Your faithfulness and have somebody scoot up and say, 'Hi, let me tow your car to the shop, and fix your tire. Here is twenty bucks for lunch."*

Or how about we say: *"Is God going to use this? Maybe the person who stops to help me needs to know that He loves them?"*

But He said to me, "My grace is sufficient for you, for My power is made perfect in weakness." Therefore I will boast all the more gladly about my weaknesses, so that Christ's power may rest on me. That is why, for Christ's sake, I delight in weaknesses, in insults, in hardships, in persecutions, in difficulties. For when I am weak, then I am strong."
2 Corinthians 12:9-10

Each day is one in a lifetime. Never again do we get to live it, so we must live each day with expectancy that God is going to do something **in** us and **through** us. This is a different perspective that only happens when we prioritize our First Love.

"Seek first His Kingdom and His righteousness, and ..." – and what? – *"all these things will be added to you."* The key is seeking **first** the Kingdom. We often do not feel free to seek the King first ... why? Because we worry about providing for our own needs.

Trust Brings Focus

Here is how I am wired: I like taking care of myself and mine ... I am a hard worker ... I am an early riser ... I am self-motivated ... I am self-disciplined ... I know my capabilities, so I trust myself. *"Seeking first the Kingdom"* means I trust Him to provide all these things, therefore I do not get distracted chasing them or providing them for myself.

Our faith needs strength, and sometimes we have to ask: *"Will God produce?"*

> *And my God will meet all your needs according to the riches of His glory in Christ Jesus.*
> **Philippians 4:19**

Prioritizing God as our First Love is the first step to sustaining 365 Days. Who would we rather depend on, God or ourselves? This is a conscious choice we must make daily.

365 Days ~ 72

#2 - *Feed Your Faith*

If you are anything like me, you probably have a routine in the morning. Mine goes something like this: Turn off the alarm ... shower ... dress ... head downstairs for something to eat (and, of course, a cup of coffee).

The one part of that routine I absolutely cannot miss is getting something to eat. Why? Because if I do not get something in my stomach before I go to work, I will start to get sick before noon.

Our physical bodies require physical food to stay healthy, vibrant, alive:

> *Jesus answered, "It is written: 'Man does not live on bread alone, but on every word that comes from the mouth of God.'"*
> **Matthew 4:4**

Our spiritual beings require spiritual food to stay healthy, vibrant, alive:

Consequently, faith comes from hearing the message, and the message is heard through the word about Christ.
Romans 10:17

We are fueled by faith. Our expectancy comes from faith. We do not live on bread alone. Bread fuels the physical body, keeping us healthy. When we are eating food, we are physically healthy. The same goes for our spiritual life: we consume the Word of God. Another way to say this is: *"Faith, spiritual health, comes by hearing – or feeding ourselves from – the Word of God."*

We all have flesh bodies. If we start off the day without eating – we do not "break our fast," that is, "eat breakfast" – then how do we think we will feel by 4 or 5 o'clock? Kind of sick, a little nauseous, a little weak? Maybe embarrassed that our stomachs have been growling loudly for several hours? So what we if do not eat the next day, and the next day, and maybe all week – until Sunday, when we gorge ourselves at church.

To stay healthy, our bodies are designed to be fueled every day. In the same way, God designed our spiritual self to need daily food to fuel it. Our spirit needs to be fed every day, maintaining health and strength, or we begin to get weak, anemic, energy-less and tired. A starving person just wants to sleep. This is true both physically and spiritually.

"Servant, Feed Thyself!"

Several years ago, God drew me into an intimate time with Him when I undertook a 40-day fast. About in the middle of this fast, God showed me a picture. It was a 1950's-type diner, and I was the waiter. I was hauling out trays of food for the customers, feeding everybody, and everyone laughing and having a good time. God said to me, *"Frank, just like a servant serves food, you are serving spiritual food."* I am delivering their orders and everyone is happy.

Then the picture changed. Although I was still serving food, I was emaciated, skin and bones, starving. I was in a restaurant filled with food, delivering meals to everyone, but I had not been nourishing myself. I felt God correct me, *"Frank, just because you serve it – even though you are reading My Word in order to minister to others – you are forgetting that you need to feed yourself."*

Too many Christians are starving themselves spiritually:

* 35% read the Bible one to two days per week
* 13% read the Bible 4 to 5 days per week
* only 21% read the Bible 5 to 7 days a week
* 31% do not read the Bible at all!

Why is this important? Answer this question: "How many days per week do you eat food?" How physically healthy would you be right now if you only eat one to two days per week?

It is shocking to realize slightly less than one-third of Christians do not read the Bible at all. *"I go to church on Sunday and I get spiritually fed."* Yes, attending church is where we all have a spiritual meal, but how healthy can we be if we only eat spiritual food on Sunday?

When God casts a vision of opportunity – 365 individual life-changing opportunities

– it must be sustainable. We must prioritize our First Love or we will default to self. If we eat whatever we want – TV, activities, games, whatever – but do not eat what God offers to us through His Word, then we will be fat, dumb, happy, and comfortable ... but not following His plan, not living by His spiritual food.

Fast Food?

We must feed on the Word every day. Every promise in the Word is accessed by faith. If we are going to sustain the 365 Days vision, we must make a commitment to read the Word. *"But, Frank, I do read. I have this little devotional. It takes me about five minutes every morning."*

I am not opposed to devotionals – that too is spiritual food. Let us put a brief daily devotional into perspective. How healthy would we be if we ate **once a day**, for 5 to 15 minutes? How much food do we need to take in? Subsisting only on a 5-minute devotional is like eating every meal at a fast-food restaurant. It costs us nothing to go to a fast-food restaurant. They do all the preparing and cooking, they do all the delivering. We walk up to the counter, throw them a few bucks, and eat.

The Word of God is not meant to be fast food, nor a quick meal. The Word of God is meant to nourish and sustain us. *"Why? So God can squeeze us into some kind of mold?"* No. God is trying to pour the love of His Son, Jesus Christ, into our hearts. He wants to pour every promise and provision of His Word into our lives.

The Challenge

"I have tried it a million times, but it has never worked for me." So let me challenge this. In many years of ministry, I have yet to hear a testimony of failure when someone has applied this principle of feeding daily and deeply on God's Word. Anyone who has taken my challenge has ended up with a lifestyle of reading the Word every single day.

"So what is the challenge?"

Every day for 40 days, we do not eat "natural food" until we have consumed "spiritual food."

Every morning when we wake up, say, *"I will not sustain my body until I have eaten of the Word. If I wake up late and do not have time for the Word, then I will go through the day drinking water, committed to not eating food. I will not eat physically until I eat spiritually."*

What happens when we do not eat physically? We begin to get sick, worn out, realizing how unhealthy we are, how fatigued and cranky. What happens when we do not eat spiritually? We begin to be confused, timid, self-centered, fearful. When we tie these two together – eating spiritually first, then eating physically – we begin to realize how much we need spiritual food! When we do this 40 days in a row, faithfully sticking to it, I **promise** we will become avid consumers of the Word.

My friend Greg had a business trip on a Wednesday morning. He left his house so fast that he forgot to spend time in the Word with the Lord. But Greg had determined to not eat physical food until he had fed his spirit with the Word. By the time he was at the airport, he was starting to feel sick. He had no Bible with him, and he did not know what to do. Then he remembered that he had a Bible on his iPhone! Greg had his time with the Lord, then grabbed something quick to eat before boarding the airplane. Centering on the Word every day changed the way he lived.

Do you know why this challenge works? It is not because digging into God's Word daily becomes a "habit" – it is because there is something marvelous that happens to the believer who reads a big chunk of the Word every day. As faith increases, fear starts to decrease ... anxiety begins to wash away, confidence in God emerges. We become sure that God is Who He says He is and will do the things He has promised to do. Forty days later, we cannot imagine living without reading the Word and having God speak through us every single day!

We sustain ourselves by feeding our faith daily. This is life-changing!

How Shall We Read?

There are many tips to help people get started on a healthy diet of eating and exercise; here are a handful of tips on getting started on a healthy diet of reading the Word.

✳ Personalize the Word:

"Dyan is shouting aloud and not holding back; she is raising her voice like a trumpet, and declaring to God's people their rebellion and to the house of Jacob their sins. For day after day, she is seeking out God, eager to know His ways, a person who does what is right and has not forsaken the commands of her God. People will ask her for just decisions and will seem eager for God to come near them!"
Isaiah 58:1-2; paraphrased

✳ Read His Word back to Him:

"Father, help Connor be just like You, because he is your dearly loved child. Help him live a life of love, just as Christ loved him and gave Himself up for him as a fragrant offering and sacrifice to You.

"Keep Connor from sexual immorality, or any kind of impurity, or greed, because

these are improper for Your holy people. Help him stay away from obscenity, foolish talk or coarse joking, which are out of place; but instead fill him with thanksgiving. He believes that no immoral, impure, greedy, or idolatrous persons shall have any inheritance in the Kingdom of Christ.

"Protect Connor from deceivers who use empty words, for Your wrath comes on those who are disobedient; keep him from partnering with them. Thank You that once he was in darkness but now he is the light in the Lord. Connor wants to live as a child of light, for that fruit consists in all goodness, righteousness and truth; he wants to find out what pleases You the most."

Ephesians 5:1-10; paraphrased

✳ Read the Word out loud:

You are the salt of the Earth. But if the salt loses its saltiness, how can it be made salty again? It is no longer good for anything, except to be thrown out and trampled underfoot.

You are the light of the world. A town built on a hill cannot be hidden. Neither do people light a lamp and put it under a bowl. Instead they put it on its stand, and it gives light to everyone in the house. In the same way, let your light shine before others, that they may see your good deeds and glorify your Father in Heaven.

Matthew 5:13-16
(New International Version)

✷ Read it in various translations and paraphrases, sometimes parallel passages:

Here's another way to put it: you're here to be light, bringing out the God-colors in the world. God is not a secret to be kept. We're going public with this, as public as a city on a hill. If I make you light-bearers, you don't think I'm going to hide you under a bucket, do you? I'm putting you on a light stand. Now that I've put you there on a hilltop, on a light stand – shine! Keep open house; be generous with your lives. By opening up

to others, you'll prompt people to open up with God, this generous Father in Heaven.
Matthew 5:14-16 *(the Message)*

You are the light of the world – like a city on a hilltop that cannot be hidden. No one lights a lamp and then puts it under a basket. Instead, a lamp is placed on a stand, where it gives light to everyone in the house. In the same way, let your good deeds shine out for all to see, so that everyone will praise your Heavenly Father.
Matthew 5:14-16
(New Living Translation)

✳ Assign yourself a word (or phrase) search – such as "righteousness" – and study all the places in the Bible where that word occurs (comparing Old Testament to New Testament is often quite illuminating).

✳ (This one is important!) **Memorize** the Word:

I have Your Word in my heart that I might not sin against You.

Psalm 119:11
(New International Version)

Or ...

I've banked Your promises in the vault of my heart so I won't sin myself bankrupt.
Psalm 119:11 *(the Message)*

✳ Maybe put it into song! Think of some songs we currently sing or have sung in church: *"I Am a Friend of God"* by Israel Houghton and Michael Gungor is straight from John 15:15 ... *"Better Is One Day In Your Courts"* by Matt Redman is from Psalm 84:10. Perhaps the next best worship song for the whole Body of Christ will come from your own reading of the Bible.

✳ Start with one Old Testament chapter and one New Testament chapter every day, gradually building up the quantity of reading as the quality of reading takes fire.

However we feed ourselves with the Word of God on a daily basis, making it an absolute priority (even over physical food), we **will** learn that God's Word is **alive!**

365 Days ~ 88

#3 - *Do Not Worry About Tomorrow*

Therefore do not worry about tomorrow, for tomorrow will worry about itself. Each day has enough trouble of its own.
Matthew 6:34

Worry is the ultimate pickpocket. A pickpocket steals something of value and we do not even know it is gone. When we start thinking about tomorrow – "What will happen tomorrow? What if this or what if that?" – all these what-ifs add up. We spend so much of our day worrying about tomorrow that Worry has pick-pocketed our once in a lifetime opportunity for God to move in and through our lives today.

Have you ever been pick-pocketed before? I have. It was before I became a Christian. I was running some nightclubs in Hawaii, and I was carrying a bank deposit with $20,000 cash in it. I had this large wad of cash in a rubber zipper bank envelope, tucked inside my jacket.

I was walking down the streets of Waikiki, and the sidewalks were packed. I was bumping into people when suddenly I realized the money was gone! I stopped, turned around, looked all around, shocked and worried. Then, about a block and a half away, this kid happened to look back at the same moment. We caught each other's eyes ... and he bolted. I ran after him, but I did not catch him. $20,000 – gone forever.

Worry causes us to focus on the uncertainty of what will happen tomorrow ... and before we know it, today is stolen away – gone forever. Jesus identified Worry as an enemy who will steal your life: *"Do not worry about tomorrow for tomorrow will worry about itself. Each day has enough issues of its own."*

Worry sneaks up on us like a concerned friend: "Hey, I am so glad you are working right now. I hear there are layoffs coming" or "It was good you got past that cancer scare. You never know when cancer can show up again." Worry undermines our joy, it starts talking about the what-ifs and the what-might-happens. While we are engaged in looking at tomorrow, today is lost.

James, Jesus' younger brother got the message:

> *Now listen, you who say, "Today or tomorrow we will go to this city or that city, spend a year there, carry on business and make money." Why, you do not even know what will happen tomorrow. ... If anyone, then, knows the good they ought to do and doesn't do it, it is sin for them.*
> **James 4:13-14a, 17**

The Apostle James was not saying do not make plans – we are supposed to be faithful to plan. Once you have done your best to plan diligently, you have to turn those plans over to God ... and it is His purpose that will win the day.

> *Many are the plans in a person's heart, but it is the LORD's purpose that prevails.*
> **Proverbs 19:21**

Knowing God is taking care of tomorrow allows us to live for today.

> *Trust in the LORD and do good; dwell in the land and enjoy safe pasture. Take*

delight in the Lord, *and He will give you the desires of your heart. Commit your way to the* Lord; *trust in Him, and He will do this. ... The* Lord *makes firm the steps of the one who delights in Him; though he may stumble, he will not fall, for the* Lord *upholds him with His hand.*
Psalm 37:3-5, 23-24

We are meant to take great comfort that God ordains our steps. If there needs to be an adjustment in our plans, He takes responsibility to make those adjustments for us. This brings peace. Worry is an entirely different thing.

Worry does not empty tomorrow of its sorrows – it empties today of its strength.
~ Corrie Ten Boom

There is nothing we can do about tomorrow once we have been faithful to plan diligently. Walking 365 Days means remaining focused on today, expectant of God to do a work in us and through us.

#4 - *Keep Doing Good*

Do you believe there are good works prepared by God in advance for you to do today?

> *For we are God's handiwork, created in Christ Jesus to do good works, which God prepared in advance for us to do.*
> **Ephesians 2:10**

My favorite part of this verse is that **we** are God's workmanship. Before we are born, there is this little stamp put on us: *"Knit together in his mother's womb by God"* (see Psalm 139:13-14). We are stamped with:

❖ GOD'S WORKMANSHIP ❖

We are God's workmanship, which qualifies us to do the works which He has prepared in advance for us to do.

Prepared in Advance

The next-best part of this verse is that these works are already *"prepared in advance."* This means the hard stuff is already done.

Imagine this conversation. I say to Tim, "Tim, I am going to give you some money and I want you to go and do my Christmas shopping for me, please."

Tim is going to say, "No way! I do not know who you are buying for, I do not know how much you want to spend, I do not even know what they want. For that matter, I do not even know these people. Forget it, it is too much!"

What if I say, "Tim, I am so busy with counseling appointments that I would like you to go down to *Best Buy,* go to their 'Will Call' counter, and pick up my Christmas shopping. It is all picked out and paid for, all you have to do is pick up my packages and drop them off at my house." Tim would agree to do that in a heartbeat because it is a no-brainer – it has all been prepared in advance.

Not As Big As You Think

We tend to think of these works that God has prepared for us as these huge things which we are just not ready to do. Remember: God knows each of us personally. He knows what kind of work we're ready for – and that is the work He is going to place in front of us. He is not going to put some giant-step, impossible thing that will cause us to stumble, to fail, to humiliate ourselves.

God knows exactly where we are in our walk with Him, in our maturity, and in our faith. He gives us work to do, maybe as simple as dropping a smile on a stranger. Perhaps it is as easy as saying, "Could I help you get your groceries to your car?" Or a phone call to a friend, "I was thinking about you today."

He could give us something wild, something big to do – and He *will* stretch us sometimes – but in every case, these are good works which He has prepared in advance for us to do.

> *And God is able to bless you abundantly, so that in all things at all times, having all you need, you will abound in every good work.*
>
> **2 Corinthians 9:8**

Not only has God done the hard stuff and prepared the work in advance, He also gives us this abounding grace so that we may be able to abound – to succeed greatly, to jump over the top – in every good work.

Active or Stagnant?

As believers, we have been born twice. The first is a natural or physical birth, from our mothers' wombs ... and a second, spiritual birth, which takes place when we receive Jesus Christ as our Savior. When this second birth takes place – the Holy Spirit comes and takes up residence within us – God fills us with grace for every good work. The Scriptures instruct us to ask God to fill us daily with His grace.

The problem occurs when we selfishly keep it all inside, using it only for our own needs. We become stagnant. Where God intended a river of His grace to flow through us, instead we become a stagnant pond.

When we keep asking God for more grace but none of His grace has been poured out to others, there is no room for

His refreshing. We begin to feel dry. We go to church but we don't get it. We start to complain that we are not being fed, the pastor is not saying anything meaningful – when in fact, the problem is in us!

We wonder why we are beginning to smell badly. It is because we are stagnant. We are not pouring out this abounding grace into others so we can ourselves be refreshed and refilled.

We become spiritually constipated, which is not comfortable. Show me a Bible-believing, Jesus-loving Christian who is not pouring out the love of Christ into other people, and I will show you someone who is unhappy and uncomfortable. They are not nice, they do not play well with others.

> *Let us not become weary in doing good, for at the proper time we will reap a harvest if we do not give up.*
> **Galatians 6:9**

If we become stagnant in doing what we are designed to do, if we become constipated in fulfilling our assignments, we need to say: *"Forgive me, God. Make me just how You intended. Now I am going to start believing for those good works."*

Then we begin to fulfill our assignments:

- *This is a smile for Joyce at the grocery store.*
- *Over here, I am practicing patience and encouragement for my son who did not do his homework and failed his assignment.*
- *Right here, I am serving my neighbor Frances who had to work late, so I am looking after her kids.*
- *Here is Robert, with whom I have been getting coffee for a year. Now it is time to invite him to church.*

As we begin to live 365 Days, we say: "Wow, Lord, that was great! Fill me, Lord, fill me!"

God says, *"There is nothing I would rather do than refresh you, to make every grace abound in your life. Let me refresh and pour into you."* Why? So we can use it on ourselves? No! So we can live out the Gospel of Christ.

The Church Age

After Jesus died on the cross, was buried, and the resurrection power of God raised Him from the dead, He ascended into Heaven. Now He is sitting at the right hand of God. This began the Church Age. This is the season of history where we have taken over Jesus' work – not His work on the cross, only He could do that – but His work of pointing out the love His Heavenly Father has for His creation, which He demonstrated by Christ's sacrifice on the cross. We do this by telling everybody we can about Him.

Why do we tell everybody about Jesus? Because God does not want anyone to burn in Hell. God is being patient:

> *The Lord is not slow in keeping His promise, as some understand slowness. Instead He is patient with you, not wanting anyone to perish but everyone to come to repentance.*
> **2 Peter 3:9**

There was a man living in the Church Age named Philip. He was way ahead of us, already living 365 Days. He was waking up, expecting God to do something in him and through him, every single day.

"Wait a minute, Frank, this does not count! He is a Bible guy, he is special. He is one of God's favorites, for goodness' sake, he is in the Bible!"

Ah, but remember: *"God does not show favoritism"* (Romans 2:11). God does not play favorites. Philip is just like you or me.

*"Phillip lived in **Bible times**. It was different then."*

We are still living in Bible times. We live in the same season of History – the Church Age – that Phillip did. Remember: the Book of Acts is the only book of History in the Bible that does not have an ending. Why? Because it is still going on! We **are** living in the Church Age. The same Holy Spirit dwelling in Philip dwells in you and me.

We think the Holy Spirit was so much cooler when the Church first started. *"Oh yeah, Holy Spirit was really fired up back then. He was doing all sorts of crazy, wild stuff. He was showing up on people's heads like flames of fire, He was shaking houses and breaking down prison walls. Now it is too bad because He has really mellowed out. I think He started listening to soft rock or jazz and got mellow. He is just not the same Holy Spirit anymore."* Excuse me?

> *Jesus Christ is the same yesterday and today and forever.*
> **Hebrews 13:8**

The Bible says God is the same today as He was yesterday, and will be the same tomorrow. He never changes. The same Holy Spirit moving in Philip then is the same Holy Spirit Who dwells in you and me and in anyone who trusts Jesus as Savior. We have the same access.

> *Now an angel of the Lord said to Philip, "Go south to the road – the desert road – that goes down from Jerusalem to Gaza."*

> *So he started out, and on his way he met an Ethiopian eunuch, an important official in charge of all the treasury of Kandake (which means "queen of the Ethiopians"). This man had gone to*

Jerusalem to worship, and on his way home was sitting in his chariot reading the Book of Isaiah the prophet. The Spirit told Philip, "Go to that chariot and stay near it."

Then Philip ran up to the chariot and heard the man reading Isaiah the prophet. "Do you understand what you are reading?" Philip asked.

"How can I," the eunuch said, "unless someone explains it to me?" So he invited Philip to come up and sit with him. This is the passage of Scripture the eunuch was reading: "He was led like a sheep to the slaughter; and as a lamb before the shearer is silent, so He did not open His mouth. In His humiliation He was deprived of justice. Who can speak of His descendants? For His life was taken from the Earth."

The eunuch asked Philip, "Tell me, please, who is the prophet talking about: himself or someone else?" Then Philip began with that very passage of

Scripture, and told him the good news about Jesus.

As they traveled along the road, they came to some water and the eunuch said, "Look, here is water. What can stand in the way of my being baptized?" And he gave orders to stop the chariot. Then both Philip and the eunuch went down into the water, and Philip baptized him.

When they came up out of the water, the Spirit of the Lord suddenly took Philip away, and the eunuch did not see him again, but when on his way rejoicing.
Acts 8:26-39

"The Spirit of the Lord told Philip, 'Go to that chariot and stay there.'" This is the same Holy Spirit we have, Who says, *"Raise your spiritual antenna, and I will take you to the good works I have prepared for you to do today."*

"The eunuch asked Phillip, 'Tell me, please, who is the prophet talking about?'" This is the same Holy Spirit Who gives us opportunities to talk about our faith today.

"They came to some water and the eunuch said, 'Look, here is water. What can stand in the way of my being baptized?" This is the same Holy Spirit Who says, *"You know you have been talking with Marty about your faith in Jesus Christ for a year. Now it is time to invite him to come to church with you."*

These are good works, prepared in advance, with an abounding grace upon each one of us to accomplish the work. Every single day of our lives, God wants to not only do a work in us but through us.

Unexpected Responses

It will not always turn out the way we think. Shortly after launching the *365 Days Vision* at our church, I received this text message from Scott:

> Hey, Pastor Frank! Tabatha and I took our first shot today at 365 Days. We were busy on the road, with places to be, when we found a homeless person in need of a shoe upgrade. We sent messages

and postponed our schedules, then went back to help her. We were roundly rejected as she would not take our help. We know that God sees our hearts and may choose to shine some untold blessing on that dear woman which she cannot turn down. Again, you followed the Holy Spirit to inspire others. We are moved to act. This will be a life-changing year.

This was my response to him:

I am so proud. Remember: we never know if we are being used to plow, plant or harvest. Sounds like you were first on the job (smiley face) - you had to do some plowing. It is a dirty job but somebody had to do it. I love you both. See you next week.

It is not whether we succeed – it is if we **obey.** When we obey, we succeed. The fruit of our work will be visible sometimes and we will share testimonies about it. Sometimes the fruit will be invisible, and the testimony will be about the joy of obeying instead.

Whether we see the fruit in the natural or it is hidden from us, be encouraged: God is using us to accomplish His will, *"that none should perish"* (2 Peter 3:9).

Remember: every single day of our lives, God wants to not only do a work IN US and THROUGH US. Keep doing good:

> *So let's not allow ourselves to get fatigued doing good. At the right time, we will harvest a good crop if we don't give up or quit. Right now, therefore, every time we get the chance, let us work for the benefit of all, starting with the people closest to us in the community of faith.*
> **Galatians 6:9-10** *(the Message)*

#5 - *Defend Yourself*

The Spiritual Arena

We have to remember that doing good works is not something that will affect the natural realm only – it will have an effect in the spiritual realm as well, and we must be ready for the spiritual battle that will ensue:

> *For our struggle is not against flesh and blood, but against the rulers, against the authorities, against the powers of this dark world and against the spiritual forces of evil in the heavenly realms.*
> **Ephesians 6:12**

There are enemies of God called the Devil and his cohorts. At all times, we are in a spiritual battle ... and we have spiritual weapons.

To aggressively defend ourselves, we have to be in a defensive mode. We have to be ready and on the alert:

> *The thief comes only to steal and kill and destroy; I have come that they may have life, and have it to the full.*

John 10:10

Be alert and of sober mind. Your enemy the devil prowls around like a roaring lion looking for someone to devour.
1 Peter 5:8

Three-Flank Attack

If Satan is going to come into our lives to steal, or kill, or destroy something to undermine our faith, what would it be? Our faith ... our families ... our health ... our church ... our sense of worthiness ... our jobs ... our relationships – all these are legitimate answers.

There are three major components to living Christ-like in the world today:

Now these three remain: faith, hope and love.
1 Corinthians 13:13a

If the enemy is going to come against us, he will try to steal or crush our **faith,** our **hope** or our **love**:

We remember before our God and Father your work produced by faith, your labor prompted by love, and your endurance inspired by hope in our Lord Jesus Christ.
1 Thessalonians 1:3

We must defend faith, or hope, or love – or all three! It is by faith that we are going to produce good works.

For it is by grace you have been saved, through faith – and this not from yourselves, it is the gift of God – not by works, so that no one can boast.
Ephesians 2:8-9

Once we become children of God, we are called to these works, called to live 365 Days one-day-at-a-time, expecting God to do something IN US and THROUGH US. We are doing a good work, prepared in advance, for which we have abundant grace. We are going to do that work by faith:

Consequently, faith comes from hearing the message, and the message is heard through the word about Christ.

Romans 10:17

When – **not IF** – the enemy comes at us, he is going to try to stop us from reading the Word each day. Why? Because the Word is where our faith originates. That is the first attack.

Then, our labor is prompted by love:

Greater love has no one than this: to lay down one's life for one's friends.
John 15:13

And what is the deal with hope?

Therefore, since we have such a hope, we are very bold.
2 Corinthians 3:12

It is our hope in Christ that makes us bold. When we are on the defensive, we get our arms up and there is no opportunity for the enemy to get in any jabs. We have to defend our hope.

Hope deferred makes the heart sick.
Proverbs 13:21a

"Hope deferred" means unrealized hope, unfulfilled expectations. We may have a hope, but it never happens – makes the heart sick, makes us give up, makes us stop pouring out, makes us feel stagnant, makes us wonder where God is. It is a sickening spiral.

> *Dear friends, although I was very eager to write to you about the salvation we share, I felt compelled to write and urge you to contend for the faith that was once for all entrusted to God's holy people. ... But you, dear friends, by building yourselves up in your most holy faith, and praying in the Holy Spirit, keep yourselves in God's love as you wait for the mercy of our Lord Jesus Christ to bring you to eternal life.*
>
> **Jude 3, 20-21**

The Apostle Jude was saying, "Although I wanted to talk to you about these other great things, first I thought I should encourage you." He began by talking about those who steal our faith – those who come in and speak bad theology, those who undermine the work of faith.

Defensive Weapons

Do not allow discouragement, disappointment, disillusionment, or despair to enter our lives, and cause us to give up. Instead we say, *"Not anymore! It stops today. That is it. I am going to defend my faith, and I am going to prepare for the enemy."*

> *We demolish arguments and every pretension that sets itself up against the knowledge of God, and we take captive every thought to make it obedient to Christ.*
> **2 Corinthians 10:5**

Every day we must be sensitive to defend our faith and not let the enemy take shots at it.

> *A final word: Be strong in the Lord and in His mighty power. Put on all of God's armor so that you will be able to stand firm against all the strategies of the devil. For we are not fighting against flesh-and-blood enemies, but against evil rulers and authorities of the unseen world, against*

mighty powers in this dark world, and against evil spirits in the heavenly places.

Therefore, put on every piece of God's armor so you will be able to resist the enemy in the time of evil. Then after the battle, you will still be standing firm.

Stand your ground, putting on the Belt of Truth and the Body Armor of God's Righteousness. For Shoes, put on the Peace that comes from the Good News, so that you will be fully prepared. In addition to all of these, hold up the Shield of Faith to stop the fiery arrows of the devil. Put on Salvation as your Helmet, and take the Sword of the Spirit, which is the Word of God.

Pray in the Spirit at all times and on every occasion. Stay alert and be persistent in your prayers for all believers everywhere.
Ephesians 6:10-18; paraphrased

✳ *The Body Armor of God's Righteousness* protects our hearts – we live righteously, and our hearts are protected.

* *The Belt of Truth* is knowing God's Word, is feeding daily on His Word, a steady, well-balanced diet.

* *The Shoes of Peace* means we are fitted with the readiness of the Gospel of peace ... or another way to say it would be, "Having our spiritual antenna up and on the alert." When we have the Gospel on our feet, we are ready to go forward to do a good work, to be the example of Christ.

* *The Helmet of Salvation* is the joy of salvation that gives us the mind of Christ, that encourages us:

    For who knows a person's thoughts except their own spirit within them? In the same way, no one knows the thoughts of God except the Spirit of God. ... For "Who has known the mind of the Lord so as to instruct Him?" But we have the mind of Christ.
    1 Corinthians 2:11, 16

* *The Shield of Faith* and *the Sword of the Spirit* are our active weapons that

defend us, and which we also use aggressively on the offense.

We need all these weapons if we are going to sustain 365 Days. Every single day of our lives, God wants to not only do a work IN US and THROUGH US.

#6 - *Do Not Walk Alone*

Christianity is a "full contact" sport – that is, we need to be in regular communication, frequently in contact with other believers. We are designed by God to walk together, and to sharpen each other.

> *As iron sharpens iron, so one person sharpens another.*
> **Proverbs 27:17**

Corporately

First, we must walk as a Church. God calls us to gather in groups, these expressions of Christ called "His local church." If we are not gathering at a local church, we are in danger of having vision stolen from us:

> *And let us consider how we may spur one another on toward love and good deeds, not giving up meeting together, as some are in the habit of doing, but let us encourage one another – and all the more as you see the Day approaching.*
> **Hebrews 10:24-25**

When we meet together, we are *"spurring one another on toward love and good deeds."* It is a big mistake to think we can survive without each other.

* *"Let us encourage one another"* – encouraging is "rubbing against each other." We cannot spur ourselves on alone.

* *"And all the more as we see the Day approaching"* – that is my favorite part of the verse. Two thousand years ago, we were warned to gather as believers. How much more urgent is the call for believers to meet together today? Our culture says, "Church is a building, a service, a place where we attend" – but I say, *"Church is an encounter with God – Who is at the center of that encounter – where His children sharpen each other."*

We cannot encourage each other if we just show up occasionally or we are inconsistent. This is even more important as we see The Day – the coming of Christ – approaching! We act like we have all the time in the world, that we can put Christ on the back-burner until we are "ready."

Church is not just a service, just a place of getting together once in a while, going in and hearing some great music, hearing a good word – *"Hey, that is kind of cool. I think I can use one of those things"* – and then walking out again. No! Please do not walk alone!

Individually

We cannot individually walk alone. There is a spiritual battle taking place between us and the enemy, who is actively and with dirty tactics trying to steal from us, to destroy us, and maybe create a stagnant experience with God.

"Iron sharpens iron" – we need to encourage each other to live 365 Days. When we leave the safety of a church, we start to be dulled by the world. If another believer sharpens us with their words, their encouragement, their urging, we are sharpened – and this can take place outside the church walls! Then we go out into the world, we start watching TV, we started watching movies, we spend time on the Internet, we are at work ... and we are hearing, hearing, hearing. Those words

dull our ears. We cannot walk our faith out alone.

We are in a fight! The enemy has been fighting with God's people since the Garden of Eden, and the Bible tells us he has a finite time to war against us. We have a responsibility to stay sharpened, ready for battle, determined to win. We need each other to keep our purpose alive and well.

That is why God says, *"Do not forsake the gathering of the believers!"* We do not want to be dull or beat up from past battles. We need each other.

> *Two are better than one, because they have a good return for their labor. If either of them falls down, one can help the other up. But pity the man who falls and has no one to help them up.*
> **Ecclesiastes 4:9-10**

The truth is: we **are** going to fall. If we think we are going to wake up each one-of-a-kind-day and never be distracted, never take a tumble – then the enemy wins the battle. If we think we are never going to come home at the end of the day and say, *"I lost it today,"* we are kidding ourselves.

As we absorb this vision of 365 Days into our hearts, each of us should align ourselves with at least one other person. Why? *"Two are better than one, because they have a good return for their work. If one falls down, his friend can help him."* We must have someone to pick us up on the days we fall.

> *Also, if two lie down together, they will keep warm. But how can one keep warm alone? Though one may be overpowered, two can defend themselves. A cord of three strands is not quickly broken.*
> **Ecclesiastes 4:11-12**

> *A friend loves at all times, and a brother is born for a time of adversity.*
> **Proverbs 17:17**

"What does 'a brother is born for a time of adversity' mean? Brothers and sisters, siblings are just destined to squabble, to fight with each other?" That is absolutely contrary to what is being said. It means that we are born to stand back-to-back

during the fight. Do not walk alone. Someone needs to have your back.

Before I committed my life to Christ, I used to run nightclubs. We had a doorman. The first rule of being a doorman in a big club is that you never fight alone. I did not care how out-of-control things were – unless the first doorman had another doorman to help, he was not allowed to engage. Why? Because the sucker punch always comes out of nowhere.

If the fight is coming at us, we have our fists up and we are defending ourselves ... but the punch that takes us out is the one that comes from behind, the one we never see coming. Find someone who is willing to call – or text, or email, or tweet, or Facebook or somehow communicate with – you 365 times during a year: *"How are you doing? How did your day go?"* Whatever environment of contact or communication we choose, we need to know that someone else has our back.

On a personal note, I have not asked my wife Dyan to do this for me, nor I for her. I want someone outside of my marriage relationship to hold me accountable. Dyan and I see each other a lot. We share everything with each other, and I trust her completely ... but I am expanding this accountability with another believer.

Carry each other's burdens, and in this way you will fulfill the law of Christ.
Galatians 6:2

Do not walk alone.

Every single day of our lives, God wants to not only do a work IN US but THROUGH US.

#7 - *Do Not Grow Weary*

The way great generals win wars is not necessarily by being the biggest and the strongest, but instead, knowing everything as much as possible of what the enemy is capable of. It is by knowing everything of which their enemy is capable that gives us the edge. If we do not know our enemy and his schemes, there is a great probability that the enemy will get the upper hand.

Paul's Pedigree

Things might not always go our way. We live in a fallen world. 365 Days is not about things going our way – it is about things going God's way, it is about the work of God in us and the work of God through us. Things will happen. 365 Days is not a solution to prevent disaster, not a self-help fix to make life perfect, not an insurance policy. Therefore, we have to recognize that things will not always go our way.

The Apostle Paul penned most of the New Testament. He had planted a church in Corinth, and he wrote two letters to them. Some false apostles had slipped into the church and tried to have some influence. He wrote, *"Hey, you guys have to get rid of these bozos! They are dangerous. They are false apostles."*

I hope you will put up with me in a little of my foolishness. Yes, please put up with me! I am jealous for you with a Godly jealousy. I promised you to one Husband, to Christ, so that I might present you as a pure virgin to Him.

But I am afraid that, just as Eve was deceived by the serpent's cunning, your minds may somehow be led astray from your sincere and pure devotion to Christ. For if someone comes to you and preaches a Jesus other than the Jesus we preached, or if you receive a different spirit from the Spirit you received, or a different Gospel from the one you accepted, you put up with it easily enough.

But I do not think I am in the least inferior to those "super-apostles." I may indeed be untrained as a speaker, but I do have knowledge. We have made this perfectly clear to you in every way.

2 Corinthians 11:1-6

He writes, *"I do not want to boast, but you forced me into it, so let me give you my pedigree, credentials, the basis for why you should believe me."* **This precious little piece of Scripture is where he talks about all the things that have not gone his way, yet he has not grown weary:**

Whatever anyone else dares to boast about – I am speaking as a fool – I also dare to boast about. Are they Hebrews? So am I. Are they Israelites? So am I. Are they Abraham's descendants? So am I. Are they servants of Christ? (I am out of my mind to talk like this.) I am more.

I have worked much harder, been in prison more frequently, been flogged more severely, and been exposed to death again and again. Five times I received from the Jews the forty lashes minus one. Three times I was beaten with rods, once I was pelted with stones, three times I was shipwrecked. I spent a night and a day in the open sea, I have been constantly on the move.

I have been in danger from rivers, in danger from bandits, in danger from my fellow Jews, in danger from Gentiles; in danger in the city, in danger in the country, in danger at sea; and in danger from false believers.

I have labored and toiled and have often gone without sleep; I have known hunger and thirst and have often gone without food; I have been cold and naked.

Besides everything else, I face daily the pressure of my concern for all the churches. Who is weak, and I do not feel weak? Who is led into sin, and I do not inwardly burn?

If I must boast, I will boast of the things that show my weakness. The God and Father of the Lord Jesus Christ, Who is to be praised forever, knows that I am not lying.

2 Corinthians 11:21b-31

Picture this conversation:

* *"Are they servants of Christ? (I am out of my mind to talk like this)"* – Meaning, "It is nuts for me to boast, but let me remind you a little about my life."

* *"I have worked much harder, been in prison more frequently, been flogged more severely, and been exposed to death again and again"* – Can we all agree things have not gone his way?

* *"Five times I received from the Jews the forty lashes minus one"* – This was the same punishment Jesus Christ received at the hands of the Romans, the famous 39 lashes.

* *"Three times I was beaten with rods, once I was stoned"* – And left for dead, or so they thought.

* *"Three times I was shipwrecked, I spent a night and a day in the open sea, I have been constantly on the move"* – Everything has certainly not gone Paul's way!

It goes on and on, a fascinating piece of Scripture. It sound to me like Paul was living 365 Days! Each day he was expecting God to do something in him and through him. God was and did ... but it did not always go his way.

> *But He said to me, "My grace is sufficient for you, for My power is made perfect in weakness." Therefore I will boast all the more gladly about my weaknesses, so that Christ's power may rest on me. That is why, for Christ's sake, I delight in weaknesses, in insults, in hardships, in persecutions in difficulties. For when I am weak, then I am strong.*
> **2 Corinthians 12:9-10**

Paul wrote: *"I am not going to grow weary and I am going to stay sharp."* Why? Because things did not always go his way – yet his faith in God was stronger than his faith in himself or his circumstances. Things happen.

Wins and Losses

Our enemy is not happy about 365 Days – unless he is hoping to see it as 365 opportunities for us to fail. Chris told me:

I was mad that the enemy lies to us and we buy into it. His lies cause us defeat. He gets to win for the moment. We look at doing 365 Days perfectly every day, but if we miss a day and fall, then we get all discouraged. We give up because of the lie of the devil.

Instead, we need to look at this as, "Today, I succeeded, I accomplished something. Today, I sowed some seed, I advanced the Kingdom one more step." We get to enjoy it. The Lord blesses it, and we get to enjoy that blessing. We get to steal it back from the enemy.

Do not grow weary. 365 Days is not like a sports team which has a winning streak of seven victories, but on the eighth game, they lose ... and then they lose hope, get discouraged and devastated. Each day, we must document our successes ... and our failures. Then we must ask:

> God, why did I lose? When You asked me to step out, I was so uncomfortable that I just could not do it. What was it in me that kept me from doing it? How could I have responded better?

When Life hands us hardships, sometimes we take them to God and say:

> Every time I think about that time I was so betrayed and brokenhearted, how am I supposed to forgive them? I cannot do it. They do not deserve to be forgiven.

365 Days living leads us to add:

> Okay, God, help me to understand this work of forgiveness You are

doing in me, and help me to extend forgiveness to others.

Is it possible that God could do a work in us in the middle of a defeat, the same as He could do a work in us in the middle of a victory? So why do we do 365 Days? Because we are in a love relationship with Jesus Christ.

The Purpose of Defeat

365 Days is about our faith. We learn the most from our defeats, not our victories. We celebrate our victories, but we learn the most from our failures. By nature, we are competitive, and when we take a defeat seriously, we want to know why we have lost. We spend more time before God asking:

How can I be such a knucklehead? How did I let this slip up on me? Why was I not paying attention? Why did I respond so poorly?

Sometimes the work of God in us is known more by the works that take place in our defeats than in our victories. There is always a strengthening of our faith taking place. Peter wrote it this way:

In all this you greatly rejoice, though now for a little while you may have had to suffer grief in all kinds of trials. These have come so that your faith – of greater worth than gold, which perishes even though refined by fire – may result in praise, glory and honor when Jesus Christ is revealed.

Though you have not seen Him, you love Him; and even though you do not see Him now, you believe in Him and are filled with an inexpressible and glorious joy, for you are receiving the end result of your faith, the salvation of your souls.
1 Peter 1:6-9

When we face defeats – and God gives us understanding why we were defeated, where we need to bring our game up a little bit – then they turn into joys. That is the thing about knowing Jesus as our Savior: He wants to turn our defeat into joy! He wants that defeat to be like a combination on a safe: a defeat can be just one more click on the dial, one more notch to opening up our lives to the fullness of everything God has for us. There is just as much potential in the greatest challenges of Life as there are in our victories.

How do we explain all that Paul wrote? If we read what happened to him without reading the part that explains the "why" and the ultimate result, we might think he was a total loser. It is like thinking, *"Where was God in that? If He was so fond of Paul, if He used Paul to write most of the New Testament, He did not take very good care of him. The poor guy was getting stoned and half-killed, beat, stripped, thrown into prison, and starved half the time. Ultimately, he was killed for his faith. What is up with that?"*

Our relationship with God is more than about our comfort – it is about our character and our eternity. It is about the plan He has for each of our lives. Paul recognized that, which is why he can boast about his defeats. He boasted about problems because his faith was strengthened. He became more Christ-like, and learned how to respond well in defeat.

Through the platform of his life, all those watching thought, *"Wow, man, nothing can get this guy down. His God is faithful."* That is how we need to live our lives: showing the faithfulness of God.

Every single day of our lives, God wants to not only do a work IN US but THROUGH US.

#8 - *Pick Sides*

We have to pick a side before we get started. We have to choose between God and this world. The Bible is very black-and-white, absolutely pointed. I appreciate the opportunity to preach and teach the Word of God without apology – then I can quote Him exactly, the way He wrote it and exactly the way He intended it.

God – Who is a loving Father – not only loves but will also discipline just as strongly, with as much love. He will instruct because He loves us and does not want us to come into harm's way.

How many parents have said to their four-year-old, "Stay on the sidewalk. Do not ride your bike on the street" or "Get down out of that tree. It is too high for you" or "No, you cannot play with that electric skill-saw. Those are Daddy's tools and they are not intended for children"?

Did we say those things because we wanted to spoil our children's fun, because we want to be joy-stealers? "Aw, Mom, you are a joy-stealer, you want to take away my fun." No, we say those things because we want to keep our children safe. God wants to keep us safe. He does not want the devil to steal the victory or the adventure – God has plans for our lives. This does not mean things always work out the way we want them to, but He can even turn our disappointments and failures into joy and victory.

Join the Team

If we are to succeed, He tells us, *"Pick a side: the world or Me. Pick your team."*

As obedient children, do not conform to the evil desires you had when you lived in ignorance. But just as He Who called you is holy, so be holy in all you do.
1 Peter 1:14-15

"Be holy because I am holy." What is "holy"? Holy means "set apart," not of the things of the world. Not having the world's values or treasures, the world's attitudes or choices. We should look differently as children of God.

Our speech becomes different, the things we view look different, the things we laugh at are different. Our actions become self-sacrificing instead of self-serving. A child of God looks different from the child of the world.

> *Dear friends, I urge you, as foreigners and exiles, to abstain from sinful desires, which war against your soul. Live such good lives among the pagans that, though they accuse you of doing wrong, they may see your good deeds and glorify God on the day He visits us.*
> **1 Peter 2:11-12**

✶ *"That they may see your good deeds"* – that is the platform of our lives.

✶ *"On the day He visits us"* – God is saying, "Pick a side." Picking a side can bring some abuse, and can be uncomfortable at times. God says, *"If you are My child, stand up and be identified as such."*

> *Do not love the world or anything in the world. If anyone loves the world, love for the Father is not in them. For everything in the world – the lust of the flesh, the lust of the eyes, and the pride of life – comes not from the Father but from the*

world. The world and its desires pass away, but whoever does the will of God lives forever.

1 John 2:15-17

"The world" means the values and culture of the world, our society. He means sinful desires, the counterfeits which Satan throws across our path. Everything the world offers is sin, counterfeit, ultimately paying in death. Sin has its "pleasure" for a season, and then comes death.

This is not talking about our families – our spouses are in the world, our kids are in the world. God does not mean we should not enjoy beautiful things – like mountains or beaches, the wonderful world He has created – He means the world as a culture system, the values that are contrary to Him because they are counterfeits of the real thing.

Another version reads:

Don't love the world's ways. Don't love the world's goods. Love of the world squeezes out love for the Father. Practically everything that goes on in the

world – wanting your way, wanting everything for yourself, wanting to appear important – has nothing to do with the Father. It just isolates you from Him. The world and all its wanting, wanting, wanting is on the way out – but whoever does what God wants is set for eternity.
1 John 2:15-17 *(the Message)*

The world and its desires pass away. We can pursue the world's values – all the things that we think will make us happy and give meaning to our lives – but they will all pass away. Ultimately, they will not bring longtime joy. Maybe a momentary rush or fulfillment, but then they bring death. The values of this culture, every quick fix that makes us comfortable or happy for the moment, will wear off ... and then the consequences will come.

What will never pass away? The promises of God in the Book. They are true now, and they will never change or erode. God's Word never wears out.

We tend to misunderstand and misquote the Scriptures. There is much upside-down preaching in America: *"God has all these promises and provisions, and everybody will be happy, happy, happy, living happily ever after."* Few talk about the rest of the truth, which is that we live in a fallen world and bad things happen. It was not God's intention ... but at least He wants to redeem us. While we are here on this Earth until we go to eternity, it is a fallen world.

Real Religion

I like to keep *"My List of the Most Half-Quoted Verses in the Bible."* Here is an example of a verse we all know very well, but which has a first part and then a second part:

> *Religion that God our Father accepts as pure and faultless is this: to look after orphans and widows in their distress.*
> **James 1:27**

Everyone knows that verse. James wrote it like the straight-shooter that he was. How many times have we heard it, giving us such self-satisfaction that we are living "true religion" when we care for widows and orphans. This is what God values, and we are doing it right.

The thing is that there is **not** a full-stop there, that is not the end of the teaching – the verse continues:

> *Pure and genuine religion in the sight of God the Father means caring for orphans and widows in their distress* ***and to keep oneself from being polluted by the world.***
>
> **James 1:27;** emphasis added

Nobody ever quotes that second half. "Real religion" is more than caring for widows and orphans – it is also a call to reach out and serve, yet stay uncorrupted by the world.

"Real religion" is not tradition with no life – it is a functioning faith, a legitimate operating relationship with God. It is laying down our lives for orphans and widows, meeting the needs of those who cannot meet their needs themselves – **and** it is keeping ourselves from being polluted by the world.

Wear Your Team Colors

How do we keep ourselves from being polluted by the world? Is it by filtering the things that come in through our eyes and ears? Is it our choices of the places where we put ourselves? God asks, *"If you have a legitimate operating relationship with Me, then are you keeping yourself from being polluted?"* Another way to put it: pick a team.

> *Elijah went before the people and said, "How long will you waver between two opinions? If the LORD is God, follow Him; but if Baal is god, follow him." But the people said nothing.*
>
> **1 Kings 18:21**

When Elijah was talking to the Jews on Mount Carmel, trying to win them back to God, he asked them, *"How long will you waver between two opinions? This is foolish and will not serve you. If the LORD is God, then follow Him; but if Baal is god, then follow him."*

The people said nothing. Nothing! They had been wavering for so long that they couldn't stand up and say, "Yes, I am going with the Lord God of Israel!" They were so polluted they could not get to that prayer of purification:

> *God, forgive me. Today I am yours. I am Yours, and I am staying Yours, and I am walking with You forever.*

Another way to pray:

> *Today I am on Your team.*

While walking 365 Days, some days we will pollute ourselves. Some days, we will just do stupid things. That would be a victory for the enemy. That is when we pull out our 365 Days Journal and write:

> *Why did I do that? Why could I not stand strong? What should I have done to prevent that?*

In our failures, God will sharpen and equip us. It has to start with a decision, with picking a team.

You adulterous people, don't you know that friendship with the world means enmity against God? Therefore, anyone who chooses to be a friend of the world becomes an enemy of God. Or do you think Scripture says without reason that the Spirit He caused to live in us envies intensely? Or do you think Scripture says without reason that He jealously longs for the Spirit He has caused to dwell in us?

James 4:4-5

In other words, the Holy Spirit Who dwells within believers is crazy about us. He wants the best for us. He knows the moment we pollute ourselves – when we give in to the lust of the eyes, the worldly values, anger, gossip, immorality, whatever our pet sins may be – and He knows we are going to take a defeat. He does not like it, but He does not give up on us.

I am just a man who bet his life on Jesus years ago. I am in love with Jesus, crazy about Him, and He has not let me down. I am thrilled with Him, pursuing Him, becoming more like Him. I have a wife, I have children, I have family and friends ...

and I live in the same culture that is trying to steal my loyalty to Jesus every minute of my life. One failure in the day does not make the entire day a failure.

> *We demolish arguments and every pretension that sets itself up against the knowledge of God, and we take captive every thought to make it obedient to Christ.*
> **2 Corinthians 10:5**

Sometimes I fail ... but I wake up the next day, shake it off, pray it off, take it captive. Through prayer, I demolish the arguments that Satan tries to throw against me. In faith, I take that promise of God to forgive me, to restore me, to right me, and to heal me. He gives me the knowledge I need.

Crushing Pet Sins

We do not allow our little pet sins to rule us. They will not produce righteousness in our lives. For example, in a family with many children it is a mistake for one of the children to become Dad's favorite. Favoritism produces a very ugly thing in families: resentment. Resentment muddies and steals joy, hope, peace – all that was meant to be. In our lives, we cannot have "pet sins" – because God says, *"Pick a side. Submit yourself to Me."*

Submit yourselves, then, to God. Resist the devil, and he will flee from you.
James 4:7

We say, *"I want to pick a side. How do I do that?"* We decide there will be no more "pet sins" allowed in our lives. We recognize that it is sin and we repent, we turn around and go the opposite way. Repenting is not enough – because our natural man will try to find that pet sin and let it in again and again – we need to come clean with someone else about our pet sins, to confess our sins to each other.

Therefore confess your sins to each other and pray for each other so that you may be healed. The prayer of a righteous man is powerful and effective.
James 5:16

"Confess" means "to agree with." Such as, *"I agree that I have this pet sin in my life, this thing I willingly allow to pop in and out of my life."* It is coming clean about our problem areas ... and asking someone else to hold us accountable about them. Repenting of the pet sin is a sincere intellectual acknowledgement that we do not want that pet sin and we are turning away from it. Confessing it to someone else holds us accountable, helps us stay on track with demolishing that sin.

> *No one who is born of God will continue in sin, because God's seed remains in them; they cannot go on sinning, because they have been born of God.*
> **1 John 3:9**

The fruit of repentance is a changed life:

> *And this is my prayer: that your love may abound more and more in knowledge and depth of insight, so that you may be able to discern what is best, and may be pure and blameless for the day of Christ, filled with the fruit of righteousness that comes through Jesus Christ – to the glory and praise of God.*
> **Philippians 1:9-11**

No longer does that pet sin have that pull, that tug on our lives. Even the value of sin, the rush of the moment no longer tugs on us. We have not only agreed what is wrong, we have repented and we have confessed it, and we are walking into the repentance that produces new fruit in us. We are held in accountability with another teammate. Pick a side.

Every single day of our lives, God wants to not only do a work IN US but THROUGH US.

#9 - *Always Remember: "There Is No Place Like Home"*

Ultimately, we have to remember constantly where Home really is.

Everyone remembers L. Frank Baum's beloved book for children, *"The Wizard of Oz."* It is about Dorothy, this cute little girl who had everything she ever wanted right in front of her ... but she could not see it. Off she goes to Oz, which is a wonderful place with extraordinary things. After seeing Oz and all these fantastic things, she come to the conclusion: *"As wondrous as Oz is, everything that was meaningful to me, what really has value in my life is back in Kansas."* The precious relationships – that is where "home" is. She clicks her heels three times and says, *"There is no place like home"* – and gets back home to Kansas.

When we live 365 Days, we need to recognize that there is no place like Home. Home for us is not here on Earth – it is in Heaven:

Dear friends, I urge you, as foreigners and exiles, to abstain from sinful desires, which wage war against your soul. Live such good lives among the pagans that, though they accuse you of doing wrong, they may see your good deeds and glorify God on the day He visits us. ... Live as free people, but do not use your freedom as a cover-up for evil; live as God's slaves.

1 Peter 2:11-12, 16

We spend our 60, 70, 80 years here ... but this is not Home. We are strangers here on Earth. We are not supposed to be living on Earth as this is the total point of our lives. Our citizenship is really in Heaven. We are just visiting here.

When we go on vacation, are we at home? No. Do we buy a house while we are on vacation? No. We are on vacation! We are there for a few weeks, we rent a hotel room or a cabin by the sea, but then we go home.

Here on Earth, we are like strangers, aliens. We are here for a season. Never think our lifetimes are everything there is, the end-all and be-all. The world is like Oz: filled with wonderful things ... but also deadly distractions. Home is really in Heaven.

We live our lives to the fullest, living intentionally. We have great plans and we accomplish great things, but we never take our eyes off where Home really is. Do not get too comfortable. When we view our lives as "home," we start to invest everything in making our lives comfortable. God says, *"Home is in Heaven with Me.* **Live here – build There."**

> *I consider that our present sufferings are not worth comparing with the glory that will be revealed in us.*
> **Romans 8:18**

> *"Do not let your hearts be troubled. You believe in God, believe also in Me. My Father's House has many rooms; if that were not so, would I have told you that I am going to prepare a place for you? And if I go and prepare a place for you, I will come back and take you to be with Me that you also may be where I am.*

You know the way to the place where I am going."

John 14:2-4

"Do not store up treasures for yourselves on Earth, where moths and vermin destroy, and where thieves break in and steal. But store up your treasures in Heaven, where moths and vermin do not destroy, and thieves do not break in and steal."

Matthew 6:19-20

The Hall of Fame

When God wanted to talk about those who love Him, He wrote out His Hall of Fame – the people He was really excited about – in Hebrews 11. The people listed in this chapter worked hard for God, but not everything went well for them. He listed them because they all had one thing in common: they knew this was not Home!

All these people were still living by faith when they died. They did not receive the things promised; they only saw them and welcomed them from a distance, admitting that they were foreigners and strangers on Earth.

People who say such things show that they are looking for a Country of their own. If they had been thinking of the country they had left, they would have had opportunity to return. Instead, they were longing for a better Country – a Heavenly One. Therefore God is not ashamed to be called their God, for He has prepared a City for them.
Hebrews 11:13-16

In this Hall of Fame, they were living life to the fullest, but they remembered there is no place like Home. God is not ashamed to be called our God. He has prepared a City for us.

Every single day of our lives, God wants to do a work IN US and THROUGH US.

#10 - *Document the Journey*

All through this book I have been talking about the *"365 Days Journal."* The whole purpose of this Journal is to keep a record of the **facts** of our lives: the surprises ... the successes ... the failures ... the hurts ... the times when God speaks to us ... the times when He is silent.

To make a *365 Days Journal* effective, we must be completely committed to telling the truth. No fudging the facts, no blank spaces.

✳ Some days our *365 Days Journals* might read:

> Today I totally blew it. I think the man at the garage is really overcharging me for fixing my car, and I loudly complained about it. I did not act like Christ, I did not sound like Christ, I did not leave him thinking, "Yeah, I

really want to go to her church."

* Other times we might write:

> There is this homeless man who sits at the corner of the shopping center every day. I see him there all the time. Today when I was waiting at the light, I rolled down my window and handed him $5. It was not much. He might go and spend it all on booze. Today I knew it was the right thing to do.

* Another time we might write:

> Today Romans 8:15 became very real to me. "For you did not receive a spirit that makes you a slave again to fear, but you received the Spirit of sonship.

> *And by Him we cry 'Abba, Father.'" That gave me such strength and assurance for the whole day."*

There is no "formula" for what we write – only that we write what God says and does in us, and what He says and does through us.

At Night

At the end of the day, we are going to sit down for a little quiet time, take out our *365 Days Journals* and reflect on that day. We only live this day once, recognizing its value by writing something about it. We recognize what God is saying to us each one of a kind day, and use the *Journal* as a way of asking Him how well we did that day. *"God, what did You do IN ME today? Did I miss anything You wanted me to understand? Were You trying to do something in my life, and I ignored it? Did I get too busy for it, or I did not have the faith, or maybe I did not want to be bothered with it?"*

The actual point of the *365 Days Journal* is to make a record of our lives, a historical account, a legacy. We are writing about the work of God in our lives, and leaving it behind for our children and grandchildren, for our friends and people we have not yet met.

Among my four boys, I have a son named Tanner Wayne. One day, Tanner is going to be able to look at my *365 Days Journal*, turn to January 1, 2011, and read what happened in my life that day. I was 57 years old on that day. Maybe he will be 57 on the day he finally reads it. Tanner can open up this book and ask, *"I wonder what was going on in Dad's life when he was 57?"* He can read my life. It is my legacy to him. 365 Days of legacy.

In the Morning

The other thing we do with our *365 Days Journals* is look at them the next morning. We write in them at night, recording the day's events ... then the next morning we are going to look at our *Journals* and remember, *"365 one-of-a-kind days! Today is the only day identified as **this** day that I will ever have!"*

We will look at these *365 Days Journals* and say, *"God, today is different. I recognize that I will never have this day back again. This is my once-in-a-lifetime-day, and I am going to live it just like that. I expect You to minister in my life today. I anticipate that You are going to do something THROUGH ME today. Pour Your love out in me, and pour it THROUGH ME."*

Suddenly, it is a different type of day! Our expectations are up, we are believing for something extraordinary. It is not that TODAY is going to be "better than" YESTERDAY because TODAY is itself – filled with hope and excitement that God, Who is our First Love, is going to use us **this** day!

Do you know what the problem with "vision" is? It leaks. The *365 Days Journal* is a place to write about the vision as it unfolds in our lives, it plugs the leaks of vision and memory. If we have never lived 365 Days so intentionally – so focused, so nourished by the Word, so worry-free, so outward-seeing, so well-armed, so committed to healthy relationships, so renewed, so assured of which team we are playing on, so aware of where Home is – then "vision" could become a setup for failure. So plug the leaks before they have a chance to destroy us.

A New Way of Living

I believe 365 Days can change our lives. This is not like making "a New Year's Resolution" and then not keeping it. It is not about having good intentions and making commitments – this is a new way of living. Because vision leaks, I believe choosing to live 365 Days produces passion, focuses vision, helps us see our pitfalls, face them honestly and see how God uses them to improve us.

You do not have to buy my *365 Days Journal* – you can make your own. Please, write at the top of every page:

This is a one-of-a-kind-day.

Journaling 365 Days is recording. Some days will be great, some will not be great. We keep a record, and we learn. We grow through that.

Samantha told me, *"It was in June when I started journaling. It became a daily thing. I may have missed a couple of days here and there, but to be honest, I have really noticed a big difference in my life."* There is something about journaling that changes us. We have a record, an account. We have a place where we reflect on the work God does in us.

These are not meant to be "private" Journals – they need to be very real:

> God, today I messed up when I swore at my son for spilling his milk. I apologized to him, but I need You to forgive me too. Help me to be less impatient. Teach me to watch my words, and not to use bad words. I want tomorrow to be a curse-word-free day.

Then one day, when your son is all grown up and reads what was written that day, he will know: *"My Dad really did love me. It hurt him because he hurt me. He let God heal him."*

We are not making a commitment to write in a *365 Days Journal* just to prove that we can do it. We are letting the *365 Days Journals* be the tools that help us realize how we can live every day as a unique and special day, another day for God to work in us, another day for God to work through us. This helps us sustain our vision. This helps us to finish well.

"Sanctification" means "becoming more and more like Christ every day." Doing 365 Days is going to help us get better every day.

Every single day of our lives, God wants to do a work IN US and THROUGH US.

The Jonah Dilemma

There is an extraordinary story in the Bible about a man named Jonah. We have all talked about this thing called the "Jonah Dilemma" – that every one of us is susceptible to the same default. We can fall back into the ways of Jonah in a split-second.

To understand this, read the entire book of Jonah (it is only four chapters long). It is helpful and preferable to read it in *The Message* translation, which is a great paraphrase to get the big picture.

"What is the Jonah Dilemma?" **It is the unwillingness to consistently obey God, to have the right attitude toward Him.** We have a tendency to go back and forth, to obey or not. In French, it is *"comme çi, comme ça"* – either "this or that" or "neither here nor there." It is a yo-yo.

Most of us struggle with obeying God. We may believe in God, but we have not added trust to that belief. The Bible calls it faith. We are still waiting to decide whether we are going to trust Him.

The book of Jonah is a historical account – it is not an allegory – but it is nearly impossible. What fish is big enough to swallow a man, yet the man stays alive inside the fish? Modern archaeology has now found skeletons of fish more than large enough to not only swallow a person but with large enough of an inside cavity that the person would be able to survive for three days. Jonah's story does not even require faith anymore since now we have physical evidence of it.

Jonah was a prophet who lived in a little town just north of Nazareth. God used most prophets to prophesy a doom or destruction coming over Israel's enemies, or to prophesy to God's people that they had better repent. Jonah had a unique job, probably not the greatest job for a prophet: God asked him to go to Nineveh – an enemy city – and preach repentance.

The people of Nineveh did not love God, did not even acknowledge Him. Jonah had to go prophesy to them that they have forty days to turn this thing around or God was going to bring the big smack-down. It was the most unusual prophesy ... and Jonah did not want to do it.

Instead of going up Nineveh, Jonah went down to Joppa, a little port in Israel. He hopped a ship headed to Tarshish, to get as far away from God as he could. (This was the entire known world at the time as they had not discovered the rest of the planet.) He was running away from God as far as he could.

Default

Often in our lives, we are faced with the Jonah Dilemma: the inability, the choice, to consistently obey God, to have a right attitude towards Him. We struggle to keep focus with God at the center of our lives. Instead, we constantly put ourselves at the center of our lives. *"God, why?"* ... or *"Why not?"* ... or *"You could have done this ... You should have done that"* ... or *"What is going on? This is not fair!"* ... or *"What are You doing?"* ... or *"I need, I want! Now, now, now! Me, me, me!"* This is the Jonah dilemma.

Understanding the Jonah Dilemma could change the way we live the rest of our days. When we understand what it was about Jonah that put him into this Dilemma, we can find a way out of it.

Every day, when we tend to default and our self-loving focus whips back on us, we need to learn to stop ... and keep our focus firmly on God. There are going to be 365 extraordinary days that we will experience – we will see the fullness of God in our lives, and watch Him working through our lives in ways we have only seen glimpses before. Like Jonah, we must keep our eyes off ourselves and find a way to fix them on Christ, keeping them there as we go through our daily lives.

The Jonah Dilemma is that place where we constantly find ourselves needing to decide whether to obey ... or to cut and run. *"This is not right, God, this is not what I expected. No, God, I am not doing it."* We start to have an attitude, and take offense against God. *"That does it, I am out of here. I am so tired of this."*

From studying the Jonah Dilemma, there are four questions we can ask ourselves ... and by the time we are finished, we will fully be refocused, expecting God to do something IN US and THROUGH US.

First Question

One day long ago, God's Word came to Jonah, Amittai's son: "Up on your feet and on your way to the big city of Nineveh! Preach to them. They're in a bad way, and I can't ignore it any longer." But Jonah got up and went the other direction to Tarshish, running away from God.

Jonah 1:1-3a *(the Message)*

The first question we must ask is this:

Are we running from God, from His plan for us ... or both?

God will ask us to do things in our lives because He wants to do a work IN US or a work THROUGH US. We often reply, *"No, I am not ready for that."*

God says, *"I am going to do a work of forgiveness"* ... or *"I am going to heal you right now"* ... or *"I want you to forgive that person."*

We answer: *"No, I do not want to do that right now"* ... *"They do not deserve it"* ... *"They have never asked for forgiveness"* ... *"It hurts"* ... *"I do not want to do it. No, Lord."* Then we start moving along with our day, and we think we are still tight with God – but that is not the case.

We cannot separate the things that God has asked us to do from our relationship with Him. He is still waiting for us back at the point of His request. He has not gone anywhere ... but we have charged ahead with our day without Him.

The Point of Disobedience

The answer to the first question is for us to recognize that God is not moving when He asks something of us. He says, *"This is what I want to do **IN** you"* ... and we say, *"No."* He says, *"This is what I want to do **THROUGH** you"* ... and we say, *"No."* He sits right there at the point of our disobedience – because He will not subvert our will or force us to participate with Him. We cannot go on without Him ... but we think we can.

"Are you running away from God, or the work He has asked you to do, or both?" – the answer is always, "Both!" They are always synonymous.

When we trust Jesus as our Savior, the Bible says at that precise moment, we are bought with a price. God sent His Son, crucified Him, spilled His blood to pay for our adoption, to pay for our sin. We were purchased with a price – therefore we belong to Him. We have a free will to love Him and obey Him, but never forget that we belong to Him. Therefore, He has the right to instruct us. He knows exactly what is best for us.

When He wants to do a work in us and we turn up our noses, we are at the point of disobedience. We are not only running from the work, we are running from God. The cool part is that He is always waiting for us to return to Him.

I can instruct one of my children (I will not embarrass anyone by naming names), "Make your bed, clean up your room, get the garbage taken out, and then we will go on with our day."

So what happens when my child has not done that, and then it is four in the afternoon and he says, "Hey, Dad, can I go bowling with my friends? Can you give me $20?"

"That is a great idea. Did you clean your room?"

"Well, no."

"Did you make your bed?"

"No."

"Did you take out the garbage?"

"No, but I will do it when I get home. Everything is cool. You know me, Dad, you have got your eye on me. You can count on me. I am going to do it because I am your boy. I am going to do it when I get home. Right now, I am just going to scoot out of here," he says.

"I do not think so," I reply. "Everything is not cool. You did not obey me. At my house, that is not how it works. You did not obey Mom or Dad." We sit at the place of disobedience, and nothing is going forward.

Everything is not okay between him and me.

I, the parent, am still at his point of disobedience. Until he goes back and does all the chores he knew he was supposed to do, there will not be any bowling with his friends.

Jonah said, *"I am not doing it. I am out of here."* God listened, and waited. *"I have good reason not to do it: they don't deserve it. Besides, You are just going to forgive them anyway. Why did I get this job? Why could not I deliver some other cool prophecy?"* Jonah had all the reasons in the world – but when he was finally disciplined by the Lord and came back, nothing had changed. God was sitting there, waiting for him.

Most of us have run away from God.

Second Question

He went to the port of Joppa and found a ship headed for Tarshish. He paid the fare and went on board, joining those going to Tarshish – as far away from God as he could get.

But God sent a huge storm at sea, the waves towering. The ship was about to break into pieces. The sailors were terrified. They called out in desperation to their gods. They threw everything they were carrying overboard to lighten the ship.
Jonah 1:3-6a *(the Message)*

The second question is:

Do we believe God will send storms into our lives to bring us back on course, to redirect us?

This is the question we need to ask ourselves, especially in our American culture. We often hear the Gospel being preached as *white picket fences and gardens of roses,* as living *la vida loca.* It is all good news. It is all the promises and provisions of God, the plan of God. *"He is a healing God, an abundant God – and there is no mention about Him as a God Who loves His children enough to discipline them."* Wrong!

God says, *"Wait a second! I am not responding to your requests until you respond to My correction."* God will send something that will cause pain for a moment, to bring us back on course. This is the God of the Bible.

> *And have you forgotten this word of encouragement that addresses you as a father addresses his son? It says, "My son, do not make light of the Lord's discipline, and do not lose heart when He rebukes you, because the Lord disciplines the one He loves, and He chastens everyone He accepts as His son.*
> **Hebrews 12:5-6**

The Nature of Storms

Do we believe God would send a hurricane into our lives to bring us back on course?

> *God sent a huge storm at sea, the waves towering. ... Meanwhile, Jonah had gone down into the hold of the ship to take a nap. He was sound asleep. The captain came to him and said, "What's this?*

Sleeping! Get up! Pray to your God! Maybe your God will see we're in trouble and rescue us."

Jonah 1:4, 6 *(the Message)*

Jonah disobeyed God, and now he was in a storm or a hurricane. The ship was breaking up, they were drowning. Everyone was scared for their lives. They were throwing out their valuables. What was Jonah doing?

He was sleeping in the hold of the ship. He was cool. He was not scared. He thought he could disobey God, head out to Joppa, and say, *"Yeah, I know that God may be a little upset, but He will get over it. He is a big God. He will understand. He is forgiving. He is always kind and so long-suffering."* He had gone right back to living and thinking God will let this pass. This was not the case.

Not every storm comes from God. Storms come from various sources:

- ✷ Some storms come from the fallen world we live in.
- ✷ Some storms are self-inflicted, by choices we make.

- ✳ Some storms are caused by others. There is a real enemy in our lives, Satan; and in the natural, we have enemies.
- ✳ Some storms come to our lives by others.

Do not think that some storms are not sent by God. It would be a mistake to think that *any* storm that comes into our lives is not sent of God.

We disobey God – *"Oh, He will get over it."* We move on with our lives – *"Uh oh, here comes a big storm. I better command it to stop."* We think storms are from the enemy and we fight against them. Then we start whining, *"God, why is there this storm in my life? Are You not listening? Do You not care? I am drowning here!"*

We are crying out to God, complaining about the storm **He** has sent to correct us. When we are feeding our faith, developing this intimate relationship with God so we can hear Him speak to us, we will learn how to hear Him speak to us: *"This is a storm for your correction, but that other is a storm you are to fight against. You need to* *take responsibility for the storm about which you need to be disciplined."*

Storms – Which Way Do We Run?

Out of pride or fear, have we ever run away from God only to find ourselves in the middle of the storm of life? Most of us will say yes.

Jonah said, *"Yes, I did it."* They threw him overboard. Most people do not give Jonah enough credit because we know the ending. We think, *"Well, Jonah knew there was going to be a big whale to rescue him, that he would not drown when he was thrown overboard."*

This was not the case! When they threw Jonah overboard, he went down into the water, he was drowning under the waves of this huge storm. He was dying. He finally believed this was from the Lord and now he was going to drown. This was his discipline, his punishment for disobeying God.

Third Question

The storm only got worse and worse, wild and raging. Then they prayed to God, "O God, don't let us drown because of this man's life, and don't blame us for his death. You are God. Do what you think is best." They took Jonah and threw him overboard. Immediately the sea was quieted down.

The sailors were impressed, no longer terrified by the sea, but in awe of God. They worshipped God, offered a sacrifice, and made vows.

Then God assigned a huge fish to swallow Jonah. Jonah was in the fish's belly for three days and nights.
Jonah 1:3b-17 *(the Message)*

At his most despairing moment, suddenly "Jaws" showed up. Jonah thought, "It is not bad enough that God is drowning me, now I am going to get chewed in the process. It is going from bad to worse. Was it really that bad of a disobedience?"

The third question:

Have we ever had a time when we thought God was disciplining us but actually was rescuing us?

Do we believe God could send a solution – an end to the storm – that looks like a discipline?

From Jonah's perspective, he was already drowning as his punishment for disobedience, but now it was getting worse. Jonah was swimming like crazy, trying to get away from the giant fish. What looked worse was in fact his salvation!

We need to look at the full character of God. God does not always rescue in the way we will expect the rescue to look like. It is not always the solution we expect. Sometimes, the solution looks worse than the discipline.

Fourth Question

Jonah was furious. He lost his temper. He yelled at God, "God! I knew it – when I was back home, I knew this was going to happen! That's why I ran off to Tarshish! I knew You were sheer grace

and mercy, not easily angered, rich in love, and ready at the drop of a hat to turn Your plans of punishment into a program of forgiveness!"
Jonah 4:1-2 *(the Message)*

Which brings us to the final question, which is an issue of trust:

Do we really trust God fully?

Do we really know in our innermost heart that He knows what is best for our lives, and we are absolutely willing to live by that?

Eventually, Jonah obeyed God, went to Nineveh, preached repentance, the city turned to God ... and Jonah was furious. *"I knew this would happen! They deserved to be destroyed! They deserved full fire and brimstone! But no, You are going to let them off the hook. You make me look like an idiot. I tell them You are going to bring gloom and doom, but You did not bring it. You relented. Now they will never know that You were really behind me. I just look foolish."*

He took this totally bad attitude with God. Was it not just a few days before that he had been drowning, then was swallowed – and saved – by a smelly fish? God brought him salvation. Now he was making a judgment: *"These people do not deserve this. I knew You would show mercy"* ... while he himself had just been shown mercy.

Another way to ask this fourth question is this: **"Do we believe that God has the right to direct all things, including our lives?"** This is a very serious question. We live in a culture where we think we must have it our way. We deserve a break. We have rights. Do we believe God has the right to do anything He wishes IN OUR LIVES and THROUGH OUR LIVES?

The Issue is Trust

It really boils down to the issue of trust. Do we really trust God? It is like God is there on top of some mountain, looking down on our lives – and although we cannot see what is around the corner, He can see. He knows the good things and the dangers in front of us. He will direct us in the way that will protect and provide for us. He knows what is best because He knows what is coming.

For example: there is a danger to the west, so He sends us to the north which is a tougher way. *"This does not look like God! I do not even want to do this. I did not sign up for this. There must be a mistake."* He knows what He is doing, and we must trust Him always.

Have we given Him permission to direct everything in our lives? Have we fully trusted Him? He tried everything He could to prove Himself trustworthy. He sent His Son, the most precious thing He had, to prove His love for us.

> *For He chose us in Him before the creation of the world to be holy and blameless in His sight. In love, He predestined us for adoption to sonship through Jesus Christ, in accordance with His pleasure and will.*
> **Ephesians 1:4-5**

Before the creation of the world, He looks through history – He sees Adam and Eve's failures, He sees our failures – but

He does not give up. God the Father says, *"Child, We – you and I – are going to go through with this anyway. But You will have to die to pay for the mess and restore them to Me."*

It started in the Garden of Eden, where there was this beautiful Tree of Life. We were meant to live in God's presence, in intimacy with no knowledge of evil. He provided this gorgeous place where we would eat the fruit and live forever, never experiencing death. What happened? Adam and Eve failed. So Jesus came to redeem us, to buy us back from Satan's grip of sin and death.

When we read the book of Revelations, we need to notice the end of the story (read Revelations 21 and 22). This time when God restores the Earth, He brings down a new Jerusalem. What does He put right in the middle of the new Jerusalem? The Tree of Life. The same Tree where we eat from it and live for eternity with God in an intimate relationship with Him. We still have a free will, but never again will we choose the way of sin.

Have we given Him the right to direct every dimension of our lives? Have we given Him access to direct our finances, our relationships, our careers? Have we given Him our past hurts, and our futures?

Then God said to Jonah, "What right do you have to get angry about this shade tree?"

Jonah said, "[I have] plenty of right! It's made me angry enough to die!"

God said, "What's this? How is it that you can change your feelings from pleasure to anger overnight about a mere shade tree that you did nothing to get? You neither planted nor watered it. It grew up one night and died the next.

"So, why can't I likewise change what I feel about Nineveh from anger to pleasure, this big city of more than 120,000 childlike people who don't yet know right from wrong, to say nothing of all the innocent animals?"

Jonah 4:9-11 *(the Message)*

Do we have the right to get angry at God over every little or big thing in our lives, like somehow He is responsible for it? God was saying, *"Jonah, what are you doing? How is it that you can change your feelings from pleasure to anger overnight?"* Has He earned the right to direct our lives? Has He not proven His trustworthiness by sending His Son, His most precious thing? Has He not proven Himself by telling us that there are going to be trials? It is not all sunny-side-up, not all *white picket fences and gardens of roses.*

> *"I have told you these things so that in Me you may have peace. In this world you **WILL** have trouble. But take heart! I have overcome the world."*
> **John 16:33;** emphasis added

God's Plan For Our Lives

This is what God says:

"There are going to be trials in your life if you are going to be My child. You are going to be persecuted if you are My child. Jesus now sits at My

right hand, and He left so you would take over for Him.

"It is going to cost you something. It is not about pleasure, or every answer to your prayers, it is not about your wants or comforts. It has never been about those.

"I am not going to heal you every time. I have purpose and plans that are greater than a mere physical healing. I have a brand-new body for you in eternity, one that will never suffer pain or death. This shell gets discarded. Wait until you see the new body I have for you!

"Jesus instructed you, 'Now take up your cross and follow Me' (Luke 9:23). *That is My plan for you."*

Calvary's cross was an instrument of death. It is not a code of ethics that we, as Christians, live by. Did not God tell us that if we are going to love Him and follow Him, if we are going to allow Him to direct our lives, that He would require us to live like Christ did – to shove that cross into the ground and lay down our lives for those around us?

Living 365 Days For Eternity

There is more at stake here than our comfort – there is the eternity of all those around us on whom we influence. Have we really given God the right to direct all things, including our lives? He has earned our trust.

He has this adventure set before us. It is not going to be an adventure where the only thing that happens to us are *white picket fences and gardens of roses: "Promises, provisions, blessings, and good times ahead!"* In the fullness of God's plan, the fullness of His character, His love, His expectations of those who follow Him, in the fullness of His Word that is preached without compromise – then we will see His character, and we will truly trust Him.

If we do not unconditionally trust Him, we will never live 365 Days, expecting a work to be done IN US and THROUGH US.

On the tragic day of September 11, 2001, people flocked to the churches, crying for help. Years later, when the recession hit, what did they do? They ran from the churches because they misunderstood the Gospel. *"God, where are we in this? Have You abandoned us? What have we done for You to forsake us?"* People were living so much for themselves, expecting so much of God's goodness and graciousness, that they forgot about the rest of the mission. When catastrophe struck, their faith was undermined, and they were left reeling.

We must take full responsibility for what it means to be a child of God. We must be willing to walk in the place of Christ, to live a Christ-like life of sacrifice. We can believe God will make every provision and promise for us, every bit of His Word to use – but not without trusting that He has the right to direct our lives for the greater purpose.

> *The Lord is not slow in keeping His promise, as some understand slowness. Instead, He is patient with you, not wanting anyone to perish, but everyone to come to repentance.*

2 Peter 3:9

The greater purpose is that none should perish but all come to a saving knowledge of Jesus Christ. The greater purpose is restoring His creation from the First Garden to the Second Garden.

Jesus is coming back for His glorious Bride – a glorious Bride who looks like Christ. One thing that makes us "like Christ" is the free will God has given us to decide for ourselves. There is no value in love unless we have the free will to choose to love. There is no value in obedience if it is done begrudgingly. Choose to live 365 Days with a grateful heart.

Begin every one of a kind day with your spiritual antenna raised, asking God sincerely, **"What do You want to do IN ME and THROUGH ME today?"**

Postscript

For the New Believer

It would be presumptuous for me to think everyone reading this book will all be believers in Jesus Christ as their Savior and Lord. If you have been stirred in your heart by a desire to begin to walk with God, this is your time! It is simple – pray this prayer in sincerity, aloud:

> God, I realize I am not part of Your Family. There are things I have done, things I have thought, parts of my life that are filled with sin. I ask You to forgive me of my sins and help me to walk out of that life and into a relationship with You.
>
> I believe Your Son Jesus Christ died for my sins, and only He can wash them all away. Right now, I accept You into my heart. Make me a new person, and help me learn how to walk 365 Days every day of my life. I am on Your team! Thank You. Amen.

The next step is to tell someone else what you have done – your best option would be to find a local Bible-believing church. These people will become your new spiritual family, people who are willing to help you walk in this new life, to grow as a believer in Jesus Christ.

I encourage you to get a Bible and start reading the Gospel of John. The story of the life of Jesus is guaranteed to show us God on Earth!

You can contact me at www.365-days.org. I will be thrilled to count you as my newest sibling in the Family of God!

For the Tired-Out Believer

I would be also remiss if I did not recognize that some may be reading this book and have been walking with Jesus Christ for many years – perhaps your whole life – but have found yourself struggling to live really alive. Each day is a hardship, not an exciting adventure with your spiritual antenna raised. Maybe you have even misplaced your spiritual antenna altogether. Pray this with me:

God, help me wake up to You! I invite You to come into my heart in a new way, to restore that First Love which has melted away, and to give me a fresh, exciting love for You. I know You have never moved farther away from me than my next breath, yet I have cobwebs and rust blocking my way back into Your arms. I give You permission to clean house, helping me identify bad habits and shortcuts which I have developed in my relationship with You.

Energize me right now to learn to live 365 Days, knowing each day is a precious gift from You, filled with opportunities for You to move THROUGH ME, enriching me, and giving me unexpected, even unusual, opportunities for You to move THROUGH ME, and bless others. Thank You, Lord, that You never gave up on me. I choose You, my First Love, today and forever! Amen.

Good job! Now do you feel that little ember inside your heart start to flicker with the fire of Life? Blow on it! Give it some oxygen! Run – do not walk – to God's Word and dive in to eat fresh bread. Maybe start with reading the Book of Acts, and see if you can relate to any of those believers who started living 365 Days on the Day of Pentecost.

Get back to me – I want to hear your story too! Contact me through my website: www.365-days.org I need to know who you are so we can both say, "I have got your back!" You can do it!

Thanks, my friend.

Acknowledgements

I would like to deeply thank those who have been a part of *365 DAYS*. You have inspired me, helped me, encouraged me, believed in me, sacrificed for me, invested in me, and – at times – put up with me (smile) to bring this book to life.

- ★ **Gary Hamner:** The book started as a twinkle in your eye before it was a twinkle in mine.
- ★ **Jeanne Halsey:** Dear friend, you have believed in me since the beginning, all those years ago. Thanks for not giving up.
- ★ **Marisa Nyman:** When the message of this book impacted you – one of the Godliest women I know – it inspired me that it was worthy of finishing.
- ★ **Andrew Phillip:** Your creative genius and insight is a gift to me.
- ★ **Kelly Young:** Thank you for knowing me well enough to trust me with your honest opinion. The book is better for it.

I love you all!

Dedication

I would like to dedicate this book to the one who I see living *365 DAYS* every day: my wife.

★ **Dyan:** Your commitment to Christ led me to challenge His claims. Your devotion to living a life of love gave me a glimpse of His. Your joy and peace showed me something I couldn't live without. Thank you for loving Christ more than you loved me. It changed my life, it changed my eternity, it changes the way I live every day. I love you.

About the Author

Frank Colacurcio is founder and leader of *Mosaic Christian Church* in Rocklin, California. Frank spent many years traveling across the United States, Canada, South America, and Africa, as an evangelist spreading the Gospel of Jesus Christ, until finally fulfilling a call to become the pastor of a local church. Since starting *Mosaic* in 2003, Frank has led this vibrant body of believers to *"Build God's Kingdom, One Life at a Time"* by reaching out to the lost, and living each day as though they will never get it back again.

After Jesus Christ, Frank is most passionate about his best friend and wife, whom he married in 1984: Dyan. Their six children are Brook Marie, Bryce William, Tanner Wayne, Annalee, Conner Jeremiah, and Jade Gabriel; they also have nine grandchildren. The Colacurcio family lives in Roseville, California.

The Editor

Jeanne Halsey is an accomplished writer, having worked for Christian ministries and secular individuals and corporations for over 30 years, ghostwriting dozens of books, articles and commentaries.

She has published many books under her own byline; she also enjoys teaching *The School of Creative Christian Writing,* helping others unlock their God-given gift of writing. Frank Colacurcio has been a dear friend of her family since 1989, and it is her delight to help him publish books that will change the world for Christ.

Jeanne and her husband Kenneth Halsey live in Blaine, Washington; they have two married children and five grandchildren. The Halseys are active members of *North County Christ the King Community Church* in Lynden, Washington. Jeanne can be reached at: halseywrite@comcast.net; or go to: www.halseywrite.com Her publications may be found at: www.lulu.com

Other Titles
By Frank Colacurcio

- *Restoration Conference Workbook*
- *365 Days*
- *365 Days Journals: Volumes 1, 2, 3, and 4*
- *Wilderness Survivor*
- *Reflections From a Hillside*
- *Fool's Gold*
- *Some Baggage Was Not Meant to Be Claimed*

By Jeanne Halsey

- *Shame-Free*
- *What's That You Have In Your Hands?*
- *3 Strikes!*
- *The Legacy of Writing*
- *The Legacy of Writing: For Kids*
- *Another Chance*
- *And God Created Theatre*
- *Messiah! Bright Morning Star: The Stage Play*
- *Stubborn Faith: Celebrating Joyce Gossett*
- *Great Transactions of the Power of God: The William Canada Shackelford Story*

* *Unlimited Potential In Christ* for Kim Ryan
* *GOD 101* for Kurt Langstraat
* *A Christmas Fantasy for Jude and Ava*
* *Another Christmas Fantasy for Jude, Ava and Aja*
* *A Bible Adventure Fantasy for Jude, Ava, Aja, and Hayley*

365 Days ~ 219

365 Days ~ 221

Made in the USA
Middletown, DE
25 June 2015